W9-ADX-663

The Big Catch

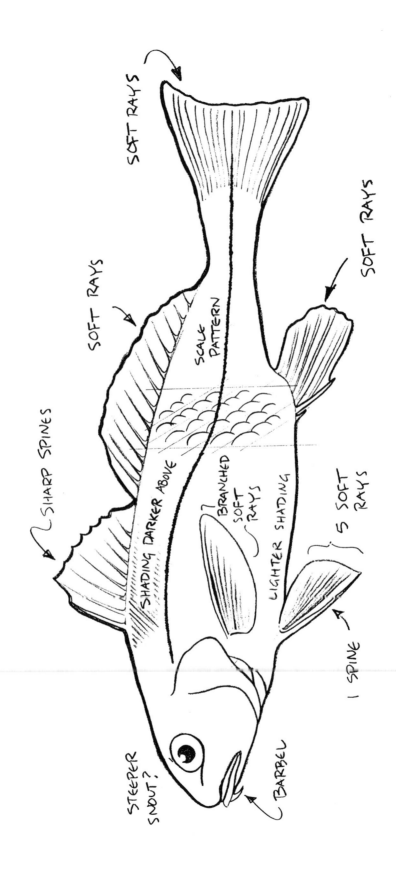

SOFT RAYS

SOFT RAYS

SOFT RAYS

SHARP SPINES

SCALE PATTERN

SHADING DARKER ABOVE

BRANCHED SOFT RAYS

LIGHTER SHADING

5 SOFT RAYS

1 SPINE

STEEPER SNOUT?

BARBEL

THE BIG CATCH

A Practical Introduction to Development

A. F. Robertson

WestviewPress

A Division of HarperCollinsPublishers

Published in 1995 in the United States of America by Westview Press, Inc., 5500 Central Avenue, Boulder, Colorado 80301-2877, and in the United Kingdom by Westview Press, 12 Hid's Copse Road, Cumnor Hill, Oxford OX2 9JJ

Library of Congress Cataloging-in-Publication Data
Robertson, A. F.
   The big catch : a practical introduction to development / A.F. Robertson
      p.   cm.
   Includes bibliographical references
   ISBN 0-8133-2521-8 — ISBN 0-8133-2522-6 (pbk.)
   1. Economic development   2. Economic development—Social aspects
I. Title.
HD75.R633   1995
338.9—dc20   95-20155
                                                               CIP

Printed and bound in the United States of America

10   9   8   7   6   5   4   3   2   1

Contents

PART TWO: PROPOSALS

PART THREE: THE EXERCISE

Acknowledgments

Many people have had a hand in shaping and reshaping these materials, but none of them can be blamed for its imperfections. My original and most prominent debt is to Professor Valpy FitzGerald, now at Queen Elizabeth House, Oxford University, and the Institute of Social Studies at The Hague. The evolution of the exercise has depended on the enthusiasm and good sportsmanship of students from some seventy countries around the world. Three recent players, Laura Aldrich, Juan Gamella, and Stephen Murray, made notable contributions to the logic and editing of this version of the exercise. For technical assistance in composing this edition, I am especially grateful to Douglas Morgan for inspecting the economic rationales, to Al Ebeling for specifying the form and habits of *Goleta bonita*, and to Brian Fagan for a memorable guided tour of fishing vessels. The map and most of the diagrams and logos were drawn by Dirk Brandts, a graphic artist with a real talent for entering into the spirit of the fiction. Francesca Bray has lived with me and my fantasies for many years, reading, advising, challenging at all stages. My sincere thanks to them all.

A. F. Robertson

A Note on
Weights and Measures

Arcadia, like most other modern countries, uses the metric system.

A yard is a little short of 1 meter, and there are 1,609 meters to the mile. A kilometer is about three-fifths (0.621) of a mile, or 1,093 yards. To convert kilometers to miles, a simple rule is to multiply by 5 and divide by 8.

A pound is a little less than half (0.454) of a kilogram.

A metric ton of 1,000 kilograms is 205 pounds heavier than a standard U.S. "short" ton of 2,000 pounds. The metric ton, however, is 35 pounds *lighter* than the British standard "long" ton of 2,240 pounds.

Alert mathematicians will note that the working year in these documents consists of fifty weeks. This follows the conventional assumption that Arcadians take a day off now and then.

Forward Upward Outward

INTRODUCTION

The Arcadian Argus

COASTAL VILLAGES BRACE THEMSELVES FOR TRANSFORMATION

The citizens of Alpha and Beta in Kappa District assembled yesterday afternoon to hear proposals that would change their lives completely.

A three-man delegation from the Central Planning Commission submitted themselves to a barrage of questions from an excited crowd gathered on the soccer pitch at Alpha.

In the same arena the previous night, the two communities faced off in the annual soccer derby. Beta gave Alpha a 3-1 drubbing. Passions were still running high.

The crowd heard proposals to buy new fishing boats and build a harbor. If plans are approved, the villages will soon be producing five times more fish, bringing a flow of cash to these very poor villages.

Who should get their hands on this windfall was the subject of strenuous discussion. Two men were taken into custody for unruly behavior.

Plans for Alpha and Beta will now be passed to the new development think tank set up by the President earlier this year. The task of SPAC — the Special Projects Advisory Committee — is to bring a touch of common sense to regional development efforts in Arcadia.

The government hopes that this showpiece project will become a model for other communities along the Arcadian coast.

Introduction

Welcome to the literal reality of the Alpha-Beta project!

Here is an opportunity to come to grips with the practical issues confronting planners and ordinary people in the pursuit of economic and social development.

The government of Arcadia proposes to modernize the fishing fleet in two coastal communities and build a factory that will produce frozen fillets for the national and export market. The Planning Commission is now asking its Special Projects Committee—of which you are a member—to decide whether the plan should go ahead and, if so, how it should be implemented.

What will happen to the old fishing boats, and who should own the new ones? Will local rivalries and vested interests jeopardize the success of the project? Will women be winners or losers? What does "development" actually mean to everyone involved, from the president of Arcadia to local teenagers, and to *you*?

The Alpha-Beta project weaves a wide range of ideas and experiences from around the real world into a vivid, synthetic case study. Its voices draw you into current arguments about the meanings of progress, inviting you to take a stand on how change should be organized and who should benefit.

History of the Exercise

This case is a complete fiction: It is not modeled on any particular country, organization, community, project, or person. Of course, the purpose of the book is to make the fiction seem as *real* as possible, and to that extent aspects of numerous "real" countries, organizations, communities, projects, and persons have found their way into these documents.

The Alpha-Beta project dates back more than twenty years to teaching in development studies at Cambridge University. With my colleague

E.V.K. FitzGerald, I developed an exercise that brought economic and social considerations together in a group decisionmaking game extending over several sessions. Our diploma and master's candidates were mainly senior administrators from countries as diverse as India, Samoa, Nigeria, and Mexico. They were the most alert and demanding of students, and the early editions of the exercise were put through some vigorous tests of plausibility and performance.[1]

The documents were put together in a playful way. In various editions the names of the fish, the president, or the director of the Planning Commission were adapted to passing circumstances and personalities. Most of the wicked puns have been purged from this version, although the name of the country still pays tribute to our Cambridge colleague Brian Van Arkadie. I brought the documents with me to Santa Barbara in 1985 and reworked them several times with classes of California social science undergraduates and graduate students. The emphasis has always been interdisciplinary, although in the fifteen years since FitzGerald and I went our separate ways, the versions that have developed in my charge have become more sociological in emphasis.

The format owes something to a marvel I discovered one rainy afternoon in my aunt's house in England when I was a child. It was a detective story published in the form of a box of documents. It began with a letter on black-edged stationery from Lady Cynthia, who lamented the death of her husband and sought advice about the urgent sale of family heirlooms. There were coroners' reports, pages from Detective-Inspector Smithers's notepad, photographs of the next corpse, a cyanide capsule in a cellophane envelope. . . . No other piece of fiction has engaged or thrilled me more with the powers of its own conviction. How well I remember those newspaper clippings in the bottom of the box relating the final, fateful hours at Graveleigh Hall. The contrast with my schoolbooks was absolute.

This poor imitation of the genre seeks to enliven the study of development by offering a simple but vivid dossier on a particular development scheme. The purpose is to convey the character and urgency of the development process to those who are unfamiliar with it and to give the reader a sense of involvement often missing in textbooks.

Case studies have always played a central part in the teaching and

---

1. An abbreviated version was published in FitzGerald's book *Public Sector Investment Planning for Developing Countries* (London: Macmillan, 1978).

study of development. We refer extensively to the record of projects from around the world, discussing how they were planned and implemented and assessing their social and economic consequences. However informative such cases may be, they have a deadening factuality: The project happened, and there's not much the student can *do* about it. Too often case studies turn into autopsies: We pick over the corpses of defunct schemes in the vague hope that somebody may be better advised in the future.

The Alpha-Beta project may be a fiction, but because it is unresolved, because it has *not* happened—yet—it is all the more immediate and challenging. The project *will not* "happen" until the reader has made some tough judgments and decisions. In this sense, the parallels with "real" development planning are remarkably close; designing and evaluating projects is an exercise in imagination visualizing people, places, and problems that seem remote and attempting to take control over a future that remains inherently uncertain. Although only a game, the Alpha-Beta project can generate a very real sort of tension as players struggle to make sense of data, assess risks, pursue their own convictions, and strike compromises.

The main purpose of the exercise is to raise questions. There are no "correct" answers hidden in these pages for the diligent student to discover. Various dilemmas are built into the story to provide food for thought and argument and to stimulate a critical awareness of different points of view. This is premised on my own opinion that there can be no single, correct solution to the problems of poverty and development. For this reason, I remain skeptical of attempts to draw up professional codes of ethics for the study and practice of development. We can only use our own knowledge and experience to mediate among various competing understandings and interests, as these apply to specific issues and activities. I argue *against* the notion of some absolute yardstick for right and wrong and *for* the idea that we should each consciously construct our own authoritative views. A central purpose of the Alpha-Beta exercise, therefore, is to provoke a self-conscious reckoning of the reader's own attitudes.

Composing these documents has been an interesting reversal of the normal procedures of social science. We began with a set of conclusions about what should be learned from the study of a development project: a framing of important dilemmas and debates with which the reader should be invited to come to terms. These are stated most emphatically in the concluding section of the book and can of course be referred to at any time. The design of the exercise developed outward from this core of moral and political issues to the institutional framework of a hypothetical country, with its government, development policies, and planning agencies. Then came the circumstantial details of imagined people, places, and events. My experience as an anthropologist tells me that it is easier to compose an account based on actual fieldwork than to try to synthesize a community and a development project in this way. The real world has logics that are hard to imitate, and it is a struggle to maintain consistency when the addition of each new "fact" threatens to throw other parts of the fiction out of kilter.

Shrewd readers have always picked holes in the Alpha-Beta story and doubtless will continue to do so. However, I have been surprised more often by the ways in which people playing this game use their own imaginations to augment the details and to paper over the cracks in the narrative or in their own arguments. They then fiercely defend the "truth" of these inventions against other players—and against me. In a discussion of the factory, a player once assured me that the electricity supply in Arcadia "is notoriously unreliable." There have been heated arguments about the relative nutritional values of fresh and dried fish. Some players resent the notion that I may have a monopoly on the "truth" about the citizens of Alpha and Beta (I wonder if they feel that way about the authors of other sorts of fiction). People have told me with great conviction what the denizens of Alpha and Beta think or how they live, mentioning details of dress or speech, architecture or cuisine, usually to press some specific point about how the project should or should not be implemented. People occasionally get quite angry, challenging what I "know" about Alpha and Beta and crying foul on the constraints I have built around the game.

This sort of manipulation suggests how decisionmakers in "real" situations operate, fleshing out limited information with suppositions of their own. A nod of assent from another member of the committee, and intuition becomes hard fact. Asking people to pause and to describe and compare the images they have in mind (of the old boats at sea, for example, or of women at work in the new factory) can be very revealing. If this divergence in imagining, this personal augmentation of "truth" is, as I suspect, normal human behavior, it offers some insight into how decisions about development and other important matters in the public domain are "really" made.

"Real" project documents usually lack ethnographic detail and are invariably selective about the information they convey. From the point of view of the efficiency of the exercise, the trick has been to leave neither too much nor too little to the imagination. The false trails that we delighted in laying down in earlier versions have almost all been eliminated. It has even proved necessary to keep certain aspects of the text (such as the cipherlike names "Alpha" and "Beta") to remind the reader that it *is* all a complete fiction.

The Scenario

The book seeks to give the reader a sense of involvement in, and responsibility for, decisions affecting the fate of people in a particular locality—a coastal region of the Republic of Arcadia. You are presented with plans for a small development project and asked to advise on whether, and how, it should proceed. It is important to understand the role that has been cast for you and the *stage* in the planning process at which you are being engaged.

The Story so Far

The government of Arcadia has been revising its planning procedures in response to criticisms, nationally and internationally, of the ways development efforts have been organized in recent decades. In pursuit of both efficiency and equity, it wants to increase opportunities for individuals and to promote a sense of mutual responsibility in regional development efforts. The government has decided to sponsor "Special Projects" to direct resources and efforts to particular localities, cutting down on waste and taking much fuller account of the interests of local people. The idea is that "ordinary people" should be both more involved in and more responsible for development projects. The professionals must now reconcile their desire to keep control with the need to engage the public more fully in designing and managing projects.

As part of this experiment, the government has appointed a Special Projects Advisory Committee (SPAC) consisting of ordinary citizens from various walks of life who are supposed to bring their common sense to bear on an evaluation of each plan and to deliver advice on how it should be put into effect. We may assume that this committee has considered several such projects already. For a couple of months, it has had on its agenda a project to develop the fishing industry in two adjacent villages, Alpha and Beta, on the coast of Arcadia. The importance of this relatively small project is heightened by the government's intention to replicate it in other parts of the country if the project is successful.

Basic plans to improve coastal fisheries have been in the making long before the Special Projects Initiative was dreamed up. Various feasibility studies date back to the 1950s, and the most recent detailed investigation was carried out by the United Nations International Fisheries Institute (IFI) four years ago. A team from IFI recently drew up a basic plan for Alpha and Beta for the Arcadian Planning Commission, a summary version of which is included in these documents. In tune with the desire to make projects more sensitive to local circumstances, the Institute of Social Studies (ISS) at the university in Arcadia's capital city was then commissioned to prepare a report on the social implications of the plan.

Members of SPAC have already met once to discuss these basic documents. The meeting seems to have been lively. Instead of moving swiftly to consensus about what should happen in Alpha and Beta, they agreed to break up into four working groups and prepare different proposals. These four reports are now being circulated for further discussion at the next meeting of SPAC.

This Is Where You Come In

You have just been appointed by the president's office to fill a vacancy in SPAC, and the director of the Central Planning Commission's Regional Projects Division has sent you a package of documents to bring you up-to-date on the committee's business. You are supposed to study them and present yourself as a new member of SPAC at its forthcoming meeting. It is hoped that on this occasion a final set of recommendations on the Alpha-Beta project will be drafted. Part of the game is to imagine what will happen at this meeting and how you will conduct yourself.

Book Layout

The book is divided into three main sections. The first and second consist of the documents for the next meeting of SPAC. Part One tells you about Special Projects and the work of the committee and provides you with copies of the International Fisheries Institute's basic plan for the project and the report commissioned from the Institute of Social Studies. Part Two contains the proposals tabled by the four subgroups for the forthcoming meeting of SPAC. The final part offers guidance on how to tackle the exercise. It is followed by a basic Reading Guide keyed to the main issues raised in the exercise.

A few additional items are scattered among these documents: clippings from Arcadia's national newspaper, a page of basic information about Arcadia from an international directory. The most substantial of these is a chapter from a travel book describing a visit to Alpha. These pieces are not part of the dossier provided by the Planning Commission; they are straws of information blowing in the wind, that may compensate a little for the reader's lack of familiarity with Arcadian affairs. It is fair to assume that

SPAC members do not operate in a vacuum but bring some knowledge of local circumstances to bear on the committee's business and that in this you may be at some disadvantage. But remember that casual information is not necessarily useful in committee deliberations: If I happen to have a cousin living in Alpha, this may be as likely to diminish my credibility in SPAC's discussions as to enhance it. An opinion derived from a magazine article you picked up will probably cut less ice than one derived assiduously from the official documents that committee members have on the table in front of them.

The Book as a Teaching Resource

The Big Catch is designed as a self-contained, graphic introduction to the problems and processes of planned development for the general reader. It requires no specialist knowledge, and although I hope it will prove instructive and entertaining, the questions it raises should serve as a provocation to learn more about development studies.

It will also be apparent that the text seeks to stimulate debate, pitching interests and opinions against one another. In other words, the book is intended for use primarily in the classroom, the Arcadian Special Projects Advisory Committee (SPAC) becoming a scenario for discussion in groups. With minor adaptations I have used these materials in many different teaching contexts, ranging from individual tuition to large sophomore classes and from graduate student seminars to weekend retreats on Third World development for interested laypersons. Stage management can be as simple or as elaborate as the organizer wishes; much will depend on time and other resources at the group's disposal.

It may be helpful if I describe how I put these materials to work in a typical undergraduate class. I use the Alpha-Beta project as an organizing framework to explore a range of topics that will be very familiar to anyone who routinely teaches the human aspects of development. The exercise provides momentum and a sense of direction for the course: Preparatory classes lead up to two or three sessions devoted to structured discussion of the project in the light of everything else that has been learned. To participate with any authority in the exercise, students must be acquainted with the classic theories of social change and know how the restructuring of the Western industrial economies has been affecting people on the periphery of the global system. To make sense of Arcadia and its economy, students should see it in the context of other countries by studying such surveys as the World Bank's annual report. To advise on project management in Alpha and Beta, they must know something of the history of cooperatives and their successes and failures in different parts of the world. A basic knowledge of feminist critiques is essential if the student is to express an opinion on how women should be involved more fully in this particular development project. Students from privileged backgrounds must try to grasp the harsh realities of poverty before they can offer proposals to remedy its most painful effects in places like Alpha and Beta. This is a major challenge to all of us in the rich countries who try to teach about Third World development; in our rapidly polarizing societies, a walk downtown may add some immediacy to movies, books, statistics, and other sources of information.

Individual teachers will have their own ideas about the relative importance of such topics, their bearing on the Alpha-Beta project, and how they should be presented to students. They will also have their own preferences for reading: The list at the end of the book is simply a personal selection of my own. As the course progresses, the instructor can assist students by indicating how particular texts and topics converge on the project exercise.

In my classes I try to ensure that students receive the Alpha-Beta dossier and read it before the course begins. I urge on them the golden rule of academic literacy: that a text should not be read once in a ponderous linear progression from beginning to end but should be perused several times, in varying degrees of intensity guided by accumulating judgments about what is interesting and necessary to know. I favor an interrogative approach to learning, the formation of questions and opinions rather than the extraction of "facts" that must be regurgitated in so-called objective tests. To repeat: there is no elemental truth concealed in these pages. This book is *not* a detective story; it ends with numerous questions that can be read first, without in any sense spoiling the "plot." Handed a short dossier like this, development professionals would work back and forth through the text, scribbling notes in the margins and on the tables. The book is presented in large format with liberal amounts of space to allow the reader to work the documents over critically with a pen. A nicely mutilated text can clear the way for a succinct report. (This is not, of course, an invitation to destroy library copies.)

Logically, the actual drama of decisionmaking on the Alpha-Beta project is scheduled for near the end of the course. How much class time I devote to this depends on how well prepared the participants are and how much I think they can extract from the materials. The longest I have allowed is nine hours for a graduate class—three afternoon sessions that leave students very engrossed and clamoring for more time. With adequate preparation two three-hour or three two-hour sessions are enough for discussion and resolution of the main issues.

I organize the first segment as a plenary session in which procedures are agreed upon, the materials reviewed, and basic questions posed. The class is then broken up into syndicates of between six and ten students, each charged with the responsibilities of the SPAC committee as designated in the project documents. Depending on how well I have come to know class members, I try to mix people of different temperaments and skills in each group.

In the second segment each syndicate enacts the SPAC meeting scheduled for July 14 in the project dossier. Few problems are caused by casting everyone in the role of a new member of the committee. Each group must review the basic plan and the four proposals and work toward recommendations of its own. I usually avoid dictating how this should be done; drifting from group to group during the allotted discussion time reveals some astonishing differences in organization, procedure, and style. Some groups become bogged down in micropolitics, struggling for consensus and unable to decide which task to perform first. Others yield to the authority of a tyrant who produces a solution almost single-handedly. Most groups struggle to conform to the rules of the game, usually electing a chair and secretary or designating one of their number as Zero Sifer, director of the Regional Projects Division and moderator of their discussions. Many choose to meet outside of class hours, thrashing out new proposals as intricate as those in the text. Others ally themselves with one of the four existing implementation schemes, elaborating their reasons and explaining why they reject the other options.

In the third segment of this program, the whole class reconvenes to hear each group present its report. A plenary discussion then ensues in which groups compare and criticize one another's tactics and conclusions. This provides an opportunity for individuals to voice their personal views, especially if they think their opinions have been submerged in the deliberations of their syndicates. If, as is usual, clear-cut options have emerged, these are put to a general vote, sealing the fate of Alpha and Beta. Outcomes are surprisingly variable. Each of the four proposals offered in the text has carried the day on at least one occasion. Crosscurrents of intergroup collusion are sometimes evident, skewing the verdict one way or another. Much, of course, depends on the size and composition of the class, issues raised in course work, and attitudes conveyed by the instructor. One virtue of using these materials is that the instructor can take a backseat for a while and observe how class members themselves develop and direct the flow of discussion.

A less extensive format consists of a class debate, with speakers defending each of the four existing proposals and a final vote resolving the matter. If the issues have already been broached, a single two- to three-hour session may be enough. In this context it is quite easy to sustain the ambience of Arcadia and the SPAC committee, although opportunities for discussion and innovative proposals are greatly reduced.

In the context of individual tutorial or private study, students usually adopt the posture of a new member of the committee, composing notes with a view to intervening in the next SPAC meeting. They may see themselves as seeking to reconcile the views of existing members or to sway the verdict in a particular direction. This exercise would normally come after the student has studied a range of relevant issues and may provide the structure for a term paper at the end of a program of guided readings. Alternatively, the questions in the concluding section of the book may serve as more specific essay composition exercises, inviting students to apply wider reading to judgments of particular aspects of this project.

For purposes of course evaluation, I have class members produce individual reports, incorporating their own critiques and proposals. I have regularly organized formal examinations around the Alpha-Beta project. The student must first make a summary statement of whether and how the project should proceed. This is followed by four or five short essays, for example:

- Do you regard the motor launches and the fish processing plant as "appropriate" technological developments for Alpha and Beta? Explain the meaning of "appropriate" in this context.
- Does comparative experience suggest that a cooperative society is a reliable means of organizing development projects in communities like Alpha and Beta?
- Evaluate the *social survey* in the ISS report of the Alpha-Beta project documents. Recognizing the limitations of time and resources, how could the survey have provided a better basis for judgments about the project?

The closing part of the book contains many questions that can be adapted for this purpose, and no doubt experienced instructors will think of many more.

The exercise should be useful in all courses concerned with the human aspects of development, most obviously upper-level classes in anthropology, sociology, geography, politics, and environmental studies. It should be clear that the book does not pretend to high levels of technical sophistication. It is *not* intended for use in advanced courses on economic planning, nor is it an exercise in ichthyology, marine technology, environmental impact assessment, or industrial management. Originally, FitzGerald and I chose a maritime setting for the very reason that neither of us knew much about fishing. We were more familiar with farming communities and believed that composing a case study about fisheries development would help us to keep our own presuppositions under control and oblige us to think about the design of the exercise from scratch. I have tried to get the "facts" straight and to aim for simplicity and clarity in presentation. Although the documents may on first reading seem complicated and detailed, experts have assured me that for a relatively small project there is more information here, presented in a clearer and less cluttered form, than one might expect in real circumstances.

ARCADIA, Republic of

Capital: Metropole.

Area: 60,000 square km.
Population: 3.1 million.
Annual average population growth 1980-89: 2.3%.

Environment: Tropical; generally hot and humid; coastal zone of raised beaches lightly forested, rising gradually to mountainous continental interior, with temperate grasslands on higher elevations.

Political system: Multi-party legislature; ruling Popular Progressive Alliance commands 110 out of 138 seats.
President since 1985: Napoleon Mines.
Independence from colonial rule: June 1962.
Periods of military rule: 1966-69, 1979-85.

Economy: Mixed, mainly agricultural, some light-industrial production (28% of GDP) in vicinity of Metropole.
Currency: 100 cents = 1 Arena
Main exports: Livestock; tropical fruit, coffee; bauxite.
GNP per capita: US$1,700.
Annual average growth in GNPpc, 1965-89: 1.6%.
Income distribution: Wealthiest 10% of households estimated to have 41% share of household income.
Average annual growth rate of merchandise trade 1980-89: Exports 2.7%, imports 0.4%.
Official development aid receipts: US$144m.

Adult literacy: 74%.
Education rate for women: 90% male rate at primary level; 81% male rate at secondary level.
Life expectancy at birth: 66 years.
Medical Services: One physician per 1,300 persons.

[Figures for 1989 unless otherwise indicated.]

PART ONE: SPECIFICATIONS

**From the Office
of the President**

**1 Avenue of the Republic
Metropole 10001
ARCADIA
Tel: 201-3000   Fax: 201-3131**

2 June 1995

Dear

It is my pleasure to invite you, on the recommendation of the Cabinet Office, to join
the Special Projects Advisory Committee (SPAC) of the National Planning
Commission. The Committee consists of Arcadians from all walks of life (the
business community, welfare services, the academy, etc.) who are distinguished by
their commitment to the cause of social development in our country.

The President's Office and the Planning Commission hope that you will be able to
commit yourself to several days' work with SPAC each month. Arrangements will be
made with the organization for which you work to secure your services on
secondment, with due compensation provided through Special Project funds.

Attached to this letter you will find a summary of the Special Projects initiative, and
of the responsibilities of the Committee. To apprise you of items currently under
discussion, I attach papers presented at the most recent meeting, held on May 21.

We ask you to join the Committee at its <u>next</u> meeting, scheduled for July 14. An
agenda and documents for that meeting will be sent to you under separate cover.

I look forward to hearing your response to this invitation at your earliest convenience.

Yours sincerely,

Oscar M. Nipotente
Secretary to the Government of Arcadia

NATIONAL PLANNING COMMISSION
GOVERNMENT OF THE REPUBLIC OF ARCADIA

12 Avenue of the Republic
Metropole 10001
Arcadia

"Helping People to
Help Themselves"

Tel: 201-3333

Fax: 201-3344

REGIONAL PROJECTS DIVISION
SPECIAL PROJECTS ADVISORY COMMITTEE

Introductory Notes

The Special Projects Advisory Committee (SPAC) was established under the provision of the Special Projects Act of 1990, by which the Government sought to revitalize regional development planning in Arcadia. Recognizing that many previous development initiatives had proved over-ambitious and wasteful, and had taken too little account of the interests of ordinary citizens, the Act sought to sponsor projects which were both more modest in scale and cost, and more precisely adapted to the needs, capacities and circumstances of people in particular localities. SPAC is involved very actively in this task: a group of informed citizens, applying their experience and common sense to the evaluation of Special Project proposals, and delivering concrete advice about how they should be put into effect.

Special Projects: "Helping People to Help Themselves"
The Special Projects Act of 1990 was a radical initiative in Arcadia. It was prompted by growing dissatisfaction with previous development planning efforts in Arcadia. Serious doubt had been cast on the economic, social, and political effectiveness of macro-planning, to which so much faith had

been attached in the 1960s and 1970s. World recession and economic difficulties at home made it clear that development schemes should be much less grandiose, more realistically attuned to the needs and capacities of ordinary people, and more respectful of the natural resources at our disposal.

Special Projects strive to meet specific local needs in efficient and equitable ways.   Imaginative and innovative, they must nevertheless operate realistically within the limited economic resources at our disposal.   They seek new ways and means of improving the lives of all Arcadians, essentially by making better use of existing capacities, rather than setting up new agencies and increasing the costs of development.   Above all, Special Projects seek to incorporate the interests and energies of local people, inspiring them to work both for their own prosperity and that of the nation.

The Special Projects Initiative is a response to recent shifts in Government policies on development. First and foremost is the desire to eliminate poverty throughout Arcadia and extend welfare services to neglected regions.   The Government is committed to fostering both private and cooperative enterprises, and to developing businesslike attitudes and competence on which the survival of a small state in the modern world must depend. Special Projects are also expected to help stem the flow of people to depressed urban areas, by revitalizing the countryside. They must also take explicit account of underprivileged groups, and in particular they must seek to involve women as full, free and equal partners in development efforts.

A basic premise of Special Projects is to integrate the activities, resources and initiatives of diverse government departments in concrete development efforts: in other words, to focus the energies of existing agencies in cooperative development efforts. The Special Projects Act empowers the Planning Commission to forge immediate and effective links between government agencies in the field, bridging the gaps between one hierarchy and another, and slashing the red tape which prevents a local health officer from collaborating directly with a local teacher or businessman.

SPAC/GP/018   -   CONFIDENTIAL MEMORANDUM

The purpose is not simply to eliminate waste and the duplication of effort, but to create synergy among Government departments, voluntary organizations, and private individuals at the local level. Special Projects typically assemble a package of basic infrastructure improvements (roads, water and electricity supply, clinics, etc.), most of which are installed and operated by existing agencies (the Ministries of Health or Education, the Public Works Department, the Cooperative Movement, etc.). Project management is usually assigned to one of these agencies, which then has the responsibility of coordinating inter-departmental efforts and mobilizing public activities around a basic plan (building a dam to raise crop yields, establishing a new factory, developing tourist resources, etc.).

One objective of the Special Projects Initiative is to adopt a more experimental approach to project design and implementation. We seek new development methods appropriate to the history, culture and physical capacities of Arcadia. Successful projects should be replicable, reducing the costs of design and implementation. However, they will not simply pursue fixed goals; they should be regarded as part of a continuous adaptive process based on the cooperative interaction of people and Government.

We need development which <u>works</u>, and which rewards both the needy and the industrious. Special Projects should <u>endure</u> as efficient and equitable enterprises, and serve the interests of <u>all</u> Arcadians, not simply small privileged groups.

<u>Public Participation: The "Dialogue for Development"</u>
Development planning in Arcadia hitherto has been criticized for a certain professional elitism which has failed to involve ordinary people in planning processes. Projects were devised by specialists in National and International bureaus, with too little reference to public interests. The failure of many ambitious development efforts can be attributed at least in part to official ignorance of local circumstances. As a result, the people who were supposed to be the beneficiaries of a project became its victims.

To remedy this, the Special Projects Act proposed three initiatives:

SPAC/GP/018   -   CONFIDENTIAL MEMORANDUM

(a) Detailed consultation with local people from the earliest stages of every project;

(b) The collection by qualified social scientists of information about local needs, social values, attitudes, etc., which may elucidate the practicability and likely success of projects;

(c) The creation of a panel of lay people drawn from all walks of life, to scrutinize each Special Project proposal, and make concrete suggestions about how it should be implemented.

It is in the spirit of this third stipulation that the Special Projects Advisory Committee (SPAC) has been established. Chaired by the Director of the Regional Projects Division, it will consist of approximately twenty-four members, each appointed for a two-year term by the President of the Republic. The intention is to involve a group of intelligent and experienced lay people in the development planning process. They are invited to screen the basic plans for each Special Project, and to deliver advice to the Regional Projects Division on how it should be implemented. The projects considered will be very diverse, and the intention is to augment specialist inputs at the research and design stage with common-sense advice from a panel of ordinary citizens.

The approach is experimental. The performance of the Committee will be evaluated in three years by a Parliamentary Standing Committee established in 1991 to review the progress of the Special Projects Act.

SPAC/GP/018   -   CONFIDENTIAL MEMORANDUM

NATIONAL PLANNING COMMISSION
GOVERNMENT OF THE REPUBLIC OF ARCADIA

12 Avenue of the Republic
Metropole 10001
Arcadia

"Helping People to
Help Themselves"

Tel: 201-3333

Fax: 201-3344

REGIONAL PROJECTS DIVISION
SPECIAL PROJECTS ADVISORY COMMITTEE

Agenda and documents for meeting - May 21

FISHERIES DEVELOPMENT PROJECT FOR ALPHA AND BETA

1.   At its meeting on May 21 next the Special Projects Advisory
Committee will study documents relating to the proposed Fisheries
Development Project for the villages of Alpha and Beta, and make general
proposals for its implementation and management.

2.   Under the rubric of the current National Five Year Plan for Peace and
Prosperity, the Ministry of Agriculture and Fisheries was invited to collaborate
with the Regional Projects Division of the National Planning Commission on
the specification of a project or projects for the development of this coastal
region of Arcadia.

3.   People in this region are almost wholly dependent on inshore fishing
with small craft, the catch being sun-dried and disposed of locally. Per capita
income is low, an estimated one-third of the national average, and local
amenities and standard of living are among the poorest in Arcadia. An
opportunity for development is suggested by various coastal surveys, which

have indicated that much more extensive use could be made of off-shore fish stocks.

4.   It was agreed that a small, viable project should be designed for the villages of Alpha and Beta. The project should raise significantly the incomes and standard of living of the project participants. Prompt action and basic social and planning costs are justified under the Special Projects (Provisions) Act of 1990, in terms of the backwardness of this region and the possibility of replicating a "package" of improvements in other coastal areas.

5.   A joint Ministry of Agriculture and Fisheries / Regional Projects Division Working Group laid down guidelines for a project to develop mechanized production of fresh fish for sale on the national market and possibly for export. Under a technical assistance agreement with the Arcadian Ministry of Agriculture and Fisheries, the International Fisheries Institute of the UN Food and Agriculture Organization carried out feasibility studies for the project, and made basic technical proposals. The IFI Mission's summary report is attached hereto.

6.   Basic specifications for reorganization of fishing and fish processing activities would involve:
      - The introduction of motor launches to extend the range of fishing and the efficiency of operations;
      - The establishment of a cleaning and processing plant to prepare fresh fish for wider distribution;
      - The improvement of harbor facilities;
      - The upgrading of the existing road link to the main coastal highway.

7.   Under the terms of the Special Projects Act, each component of this basic infrastructure package has been ratified with the various Government Ministries and Agencies, provision being contingent on the fisheries development project being put into effect. Construction of road and harbor facilities will be coordinated by the Public Works Department, and will be funded on the basis of non-recurrent grants. As part of this infrastructure package, a new community center will be built to house health, welfare and community development facilities sponsored by the appropriate government departments.

8.   Operation of the project will be placed under the supervision of the National Fishermen's Cooperative Union, subject to managerial guidelines laid down by the Planning Commission. Fishing vessels of a class specified in the technical reports will be provided under the terms of a current trade agreement with the Government of Illyria. Loans for the purchase of these craft, and for construction of the processing plant, will be made under the provisions of the Special Projects Act. Cost of establishing and operating these facilities will be recovered through the operation of the project itself.

9.   On a scheduling agreement with all parties concerned, the project must be fully operational within four years of installation of the basic infrastructure.

10.   The terms of the 1990 Act require that Special Projects of this kind must incorporate thorough inquiry into the social conditions, constraints, attitudes, and interests of the local population. Accordingly, the Regional Projects Division, in consultation with the IFI Mission, invited the Institute of Social Studies at the University of Metropole to make a social feasibility study in the communities to be affected by the proposed project. A copy of the ISS report is attached hereto.

11.   The Special Projects Advisory Committee is now charged to consider:
       (a) whether or not the project should proceed, and
       (b) what basic procedures should be laid down for its implementation.

12.   On completion of the project review the Planning Commission will forward the recommendations on the project to the President's Office for final approval.

Zero Sifer
Director, Regional Projects Division

International
Fisheries Institute

REPORT OF

THE UNITED NATIONS FOOD AND AGRICULTURE ORGANIZATION

INTERNATIONAL FISHERIES INSTITUTE

to the

NATIONAL PLANNING COMMISSION

of the

GOVERNMENT OF THE REPUBLIC OF ARCADIA

on the

PROPOSED COASTAL FISHERIES DEVELOPMENT PROJECT

AT THE COMMUNITIES OF ALPHA AND BETA

Metropole, March 1995

1. INTRODUCTION

1.1.   Following a request (TA 371/C3/93) under the current technical assistance program with the Arcadian government, the International Fisheries Institute was asked to make basic proposals for a small scale fisheries development project based on the communities of Alpha and Beta in Kappa District of Arcadia, under the terms of the Special Projects Act (1990). A team of three experts (headed by Dr. C. Herring) visited the project area and the relevant administrative departments last March.   The following is a summary of the full report (IFI/288A/421/94) submitted to the Arcadian Government in September 1994.

1.2.   The IFI team proposes a development package for Alpha and Beta comprising the following:
(a) Provision of basic infrastructure, including construction of harbor and road link, built and maintained by the Public Works Department with funding from central government.
(b) Construction of a community center, funded jointly by the Ministries of Health and of Community Development and Social Welfare; costs of operating these facilities to be shared with the local community.
(c) Construction of a fish processing factory, and provision of a mechanized fishing fleet of 40 vessels, both provided on amortization to the local community under the aegis of the National Fishermen's Cooperative Union.

2. TECHNICAL SUMMARY

2.1.   Proposals for fisheries development in this region have been under discussion for many years. In planning the present project, the IFI team has drawn on reports prepared by the Imperial White Fish Authority (1957), the Moscow Academy Ichthyological Institute (1977), and the Stamford Aqua-Biology Research Institute (1988).   The most recent appraisal of fish resources in Arcadian coastal waters was carried out four years ago by the IFI itself (UN/47/3001/91).

2.2.   *Fish Resources*
2.2.1.   The natural resource on which this project is based is a relatively abundant, palatable fish, well known in Arcadia by its vernacular name *goleta*.

A notable feature of any population of *Goleta bonita* is its attachment to a specific estuarine area. The dependence of the breeding cycle on inshore waters in the vicinity of a particular river mouth has tended to produce morphologically distinct local populations, modulated genetically by sporadic immigration from other coastal populations. On this section of the Arcadian coast the continental shelf slopes quite gradually out to sea for about 24 km, providing an ideal shoaling environment for goleta. The fact that the distribution of this fish is mostly confined to territorial waters enhances the capacity of the Arcadian government to control the exploitation of this valuable resource.

2.2.2. The dependence of goleta on shallower inshore waters for reproduction makes them very susceptible to over-fishing. This implies that any project to increase catches must entail rigorous management of fishing activities. Detailed monitoring on this coast over a period of more than thirty years indicates relatively low natural inter-annual fluctuations in fish stocks attributable to the effects of climate, etc. on breeding patterns and recruitment success. This has allowed the Ministry of Agriculture and Fisheries to fix with some assurance a relatively generous limit of 10,000 tons for the annual goleta catch on this particular segment of the coast.

2.2.3. The pelagic larvae of goleta are deposited close to the shore and recruits develop in the rich alluvial waters around the river mouth. As they mature and increase in biomass, the goleta range further out to sea, where they may attain lengths of up to 50 cm and 2 kg in weight. From the perspectives of both fish conservation and catch size, optimal fishing grounds are in the range of 3 km to 15 km offshore, where younger fish develop quite rapidly to around 30 cm / 1 kg. Extending the range of fishing has the further advantage of reducing the bycatch of other less valuable fish, which tend to intermingle with goleta in shallower water.

2.2.4. It is safe to assume that local fishermen will themselves perceive the advantages of the proposed project. They have evidently known for generations of the dangers of over-fishing inshore waters, and understand both the advantages of extending the range of fishing offshore, and the need for efficient management of this valuable resource.

2.3. *Fishing Vessels*

2.3.1. It is proposed that the necessary control over the project be exerted (a) by reducing the existing motley collection of smaller boats to a set of larger and more powerful vessels whose operations can be directed more efficiently and more economically; and (b) by establishing unified management of the new fleet and the project as a whole through the agency of the National Fishermen's

IFI Report

Cooperative (see section 4.1 below). Such management will allow the demarcation and effective control of fishing waters and breeding refuges should these prove necessary.

2.3.2. At present some 140 small craft, constructed from local timber and crewed by three men, operate from the beaches of Alpha and Beta. Catches are estimated to run at 300 kg a week for each boat, equivalent to 15 metric tons a year (see Table 1). This is sold regionally, after preparation and drying, for approximately 60 Arcadian arenas (A.60) per 100 kg, with some seasonal variation. The annual catch of the two communities is thus approximately 2,100 metric tons, the dry weight sold amounting to half of this quantity. The average weekly earnings of about A.90 for each boat are divided according to custom among crew and household members engaged in catching, processing and distributing the fish.

2.3.3. While the existing manually propelled boats rarely venture more than 4 km from the coastline, fishermen are undoubtedly aware that larger and more seaworthy vessels may proceed safely and rapidly under motor power to very much more extensive fishing grounds offshore. Indeed, it is apparent that fishing in this region is already evolving toward larger, motor-powered craft. The project expedites this natural trend while extending the advantages of greater efficiency to all fishermen in the community.

2.3.4. It is proposed that the existing traditional craft should be completely replaced by 40 motorized vessels operating from a small harbor at the river mouth (see map). The craft recommended (IFI/288A/421/94) are "Pisces" class 200 horsepower launches (see Annex, Figure 2). These are available on unusually favorable terms from the suppliers (Barkexport of Odetta) for A.50,000 each, under a special bilateral trade agreement with the government of Illyria (see Official Gazette for 31-5-93). By the end of the present year there will be approximately 250 of these vessels operating in Arcadia, under the aegis of the National Fishermen's Cooperative, promising considerable economies of scale in supply, maintenance, etc. for this and other projects. Each vessel operates with a crew of up to eight, two of whom must be qualified seamen. Each vessel will produce an estimated annual catch of 250 tons, a total for the fleet of 10,000 tons per year.

2.4   *Fish Processing Plant*

2.4.1. It is proposed to set up a filleting and freezing plant near the new harbor on the Beta side of the river (see map). This has the capacity to process some 10,000 tons of fish a year and produce some 6,500 tons of frozen fillets. These will be packed and transported by trucks of the Arcadian Fish Corporation (AFC) to Metropole. There they will be marketed by the AFC at standard ex-plant prices adjusted for transport costs.

2.4.2. The factory is a type 2B fish processing plant, designed and constructed on commission from the Arcadian Ministry of Agriculture and Fisheries by the local firm of I.Dificio at a cost of A.11 million. An installation of this type has been operating successfully for five years at Omega, about 70 km along the coast. Fish are cleaned mechanically, and are filleted, trimmed and packed manually. Fresh water will be pumped from the river and purified for processing and ice-making. Under Special Projects agreement, the Electricity Board of Arcadia will establish a supplementary high-voltage link to the National Grid line some 8 km inland.

3. INFRASTRUCTURE DEVELOPMENT

3.1. For the project to proceed, substantial infrastructure works will be required (see Annex 1, Table 3, and Figures 1 and 2). These are:

(a) A harbor with berths for the 40 new "Pisces" vessels

(b) Improvement of the road link to the main coastal highway and the bridge between Beta and Alpha, in order to establish all-weather vehicular access to Metropole

(c) Construction of a community center (including basic clinic facilities) near Beta

These facilities will be provided under the terms of the Special Projects Act by the Arcadian Department of Public Works at a total cost of A.6,200,000 (see Public Works Department KO/3343/C20/93).

3.2. The *harbor* works comprise the following:

(a) dredging and excavating the Beta bank of the river to a depth of 6 m.

(b) erecting a concrete quay some 160 m long for unloading and mooring,

(c) constructing a slipway for water access and routine boat maintenance,

(d) building sheds for storing fuel and equipment,

(e) paving and roofing an area for drying and repairing nets.

3.3. The *road and bridge* will provide an essential link for immediate and long-term development. It is estimated that some six AFC refrigerated vehicles a day will be arriving and departing.

(a) The present dirt road of 5.8 km to the coastal highway will be remade

to a standard 8 m width, and given an all-weather surface.
(b) The wooden bridge connecting Alpha with Beta will be replaced by a simple steel girder structure.

3.4.   *Community Center*
This will comprise a basic grade 4 clinic, with adjoining facilities for meetings, education, technical training, and recreation. Under the terms of the Special Projects Act, the two Ministries responsible (Health, and Community Development and Social Welfare) will pay the capital and basic maintenance costs of these facilities, but 50% of operating costs must be borne by the community, in this case through project profits accruing to the Fishermen's Cooperative.

4. PROJECT MANAGEMENT

4.1.   Under the terms of the Special Projects Act, and by agreement with the National Fishermen's Cooperative Union (NFCU), ownership and management of the new boats and the processing facilities, and control of profits, will be in the hands of a local NFCU branch. Special Projects take advantage of provisions in the Cooperative Movement (Supplementary Regulations) Act of 1978, allowing considerable license in the formation of local primary societies, especially those instituted within the context of development projects. To facilitate and expedite such projects, the NFCU reserves the right to appoint or approve managers for all cooperative societies with an annual turnover in excess of A.500,000.

4.2.   *Accounts*
Separate operational accounts are given below for the two segments of the enterprise (see Annex, Tables 4 and 5). Overall profit margins must be sufficient to provide:
(1) security against medium-term fluctuations in running costs,
(2) supplementary capital for purchasing, maintaining and improving fishing equipment,
(3) contributions to maintenance of welfare facilities under the terms of the Special Projects Act,
(4) inducements for public cooperation in the form of shareholding, bonuses, grants, discretionary payments, etc.
It is proposed that general community charges (e.g., support for new health services) and savings for general community development should be set against profits accruing to the fish processing plant. Accordingly, on the basis of a

stabilized ex-factory price of A.900 per ton, it is recommended that the fish processing plant will pay A.200 per ton (A.20 / 100 kg) for landed fish. Estimated profits for the new fleet of nearly A.150,000 a year will be designated for capital development, essentially purchase and servicing of nets and other essential equipment.

4.3. *Operation of the Fish Processing Plant*

Under the provisional agreement, the NFCU will receive a budget of A.500,000 annually for maintenance and renewal of equipment, etc., and a fixed fee of A.300,000 p.a. to cover administrative and managerial costs in relation to the project as a whole. The factory will employ eight skilled men in supervisory and engineering positions, and 100 women who will be primarily engaged in the simple but delicate task of filleting and packing the fish. Comparison with similar enterprises in Arcadia suggests a wage rate, consistent with the operating account, of A.40 per week for unskilled labor, and A.125 per week for technical grades (see Annex, Table 4).

4.4. *Operation of Fishing Vessels*

4.4.1. The "Pisces" class of vessels has been selected with a view to establishing a largely self-reliant local fleet. Basic maintenance and painting tasks will be performed on the harbor slipway, but major engine and hull repairs will be carried out at the Metropole shipyard of the National Fishermen's Cooperative Union.

4.4.2. Each launch will have eight crew members. Relatively high manning levels are in accord with the expectation that employment will be sustained at as high a level as possible in projects of this kind. There will be a reduction in total fleet employment from 420 jobs at present to 320 when the project is fully installed (see Annex, Table 5). Operation of an offshore vessel with an engine capacity in excess of 99 hp requires a maritime license, which indicates that, at least initially, two qualified seamen must be recruited for each vessel, probably from outside the two communities. It would clearly be desirable to start the training of suitable local fishermen in the relevant navigational, engineering and fishing skills as soon as possible.

4.4.3. During the ten year amortization period, fishermen will be paid on a regular wage basis. In consultation with the NFCU wage rates for unskilled fishermen are currently budgeted at A.50 per week, and A.120 for qualified seamen. Details of terms of employment, differential rates of remuneration, etc., have yet to be set.

IFI Report

5. PROJECT SCHEDULE

5.1.   According to Public Works Department projections (KO/3343/C20/93), basic infrastructure can be completed within 11 months of project authorization. The fish processing plant will be constructed within the same period.

5.2.   "Pisces" vessels can be supplied at six months' notice from the NFCU shipyard in Metropole, offering some flexibility in fleet buildup. Detailed proposals for introducing the new vessels and eliminating the old have yet to be discussed.

5.3.   On estimation of net present value, the project must be fully operational *no later than* four years after installation of the basic infrastructure.

6. SUMMARY APPRAISAL: COSTS AND BENEFITS OF THE PROJECT

6.1.   Modernization of fishing operations in the Alpha-Beta area promises a very substantial improvement in productivity and in local incomes. The project will initiate a decisive transformation in economic and social organization, proliferating new opportunities within these hitherto isolated and impoverished communities. Operating accounts for the new installations and equipment show the overall gains of this particular project, expressed in substantial profits to the local branch of the NFCU.

6.2.   *Income and Employment*
The improvement in incomes implied by modernization is immediately clear (see Annex, Table 6): total annual income to the community will be more than tripled. However, the project generates a significantly different employment pattern, indicated in Table 7.   In the absence of specific instructions, and without information as to appropriate weights, we have not been able to apply any income distribution criteria to the project. Although fewer fishermen will have full time employment, direct wage earnings of women will be increased.

6.3.   *Management and Forward Investment*
The responsibilities and activities of the Fishermen's Cooperative will be increased very significantly by the project - indeed it will have a substantial

controlling interest in the local pattern of incomes. This change could have potentially disruptive consequences unless equitable mechanisms for the use of this money are developed. Recognizing these responsibilities, the NFCU might consider financing (e.g., through wage payments) the development of other projects in the immediate vicinity, or organizing service enterprises with preferential employment for unemployed fishermen.

6.4. *Social Benefits*

6.4.1. Under the terms of the Special Projects Act, attention is focused primarily on the direct net benefit to the communities themselves. Accordingly, no attempt has been made to assess the value of the project to the economy at large (e.g. through the use of shadow prices). However, broadly interpreted, the wider social benefits of the project seem very favorable.

6.4.2. As a secondary effect of the project itself, the higher level of income in the community will generate increased levels of expenditure, and in consequence there will be a demand for more shops, farm produce, artisan activities, building, provision of recreation facilities and so on. There will also be opportunities more directly related to the project itself, such as boat servicing, repairing of nets, and general port works. This will have a multiplier effect on employment: judging from development projects of a similar scale elsewhere in Arcadia, we would expect additional jobs to be created at a ratio of about 1.5 to every one in the project itself. The total number of jobs should reach 1,000 once the project has achieved its full effect, which should absorb much of the labor force displaced from traditional fishing and processing, and attract outsiders into the area to establish new enterprises.

6.5. *In sum*, we can confidently recommend this project, which, with adequate provisions for efficient management and effective public response, will undoubtedly make a useful contribution to the development of Arcadia.

IFI Report

ANNEX: Tables and Figures

Table 1: Productivity of Traditional Fishing Boats

	Boat per Week	Boat per Year	Fleet (= 140) per Year
Catch kilograms	300	15,000	2,100,000
Processed weight kilograms	150	7,500	1,050,000
Sales of processed fish @ A.60 per 100 kg	90	4,500	630,000

Table 2: Productivity of "Pisces" class vessels

	Boat per week	Boat per year	Fleet (= 40) per year
Catch kilograms	5,000	250,000	10,000,000
Processed weight kilograms	3,250	162,500	6,500,000
Sales of processed fish @ A.90 per 100 kg	2,925	146,250	5,850,000

IFI Report

Table 3: Cost of Basic Infrastructure Provision

	Initial Capital Cost (A.)	Annual Maintenance (A.)	Net Present Value over 30 years (A.)
Harbor	4,000,000	200,000	5,890,000
Road	1,200,000	60,000	1,760,000
Community Center	1,000,000	50,000	1,420,000
TOTAL	6,200,000	310,000	9,070,000

Table 4: Operations Account for Fish Processing Plant

Annual Costs	(A.)
Amortization *	1,210,000
Administration	300,000
Maintenance	500,000
Other (power, packaging, etc.)	800,000
Skilled labor: 8 @ A.125 per week **	50,000
Unskilled labor: 100 @ A.40 per week **	200,000
Inputs: fish @ A.200 / ton (new vessels)	2,000,000
TOTAL	5,060,000

Sales:

6,500 tons to AFC @ A.900 / ton	5,850,000
Profit (to NFC)	790,000

* Basic cost of plant = A.11,000,000
  Capital charge of 0.11 per annum over 25 years = A.19,250,000
  Total amortized cost of plant = A.30,250,000
  Annual payment = A.1,210,000

** A working year is reckoned as 50 weeks.

IFI Report

Table 5: Operations Account for "Pisces" Vessels

	Per Boat (A.)	Full Fleet (A.)
Annual Costs		
Amortization *	8,150	326,000
Fuel, maintenance, etc.	11,250	450,000
Skilled labor	12,000	480,000
Unskilled labor	15,000	600,000
TOTAL	46,400	1,856,000
Sales: @ A.200 / ton		
to processing plant	50,000	2,000,000
Profit (to NFC)	3,600	144,000

* Basic cost of vessel = A.50,000
Capital charge of 0.163 per annum over 10 years = A.31,500
Total amortized cost of vessel = A.81,500
Annual payment = A.8,150 per vessel

Table 6: Economic Benefits to the Community

	Traditional (A.)	New (A.)
Wages and salaries		
Fishing	----	1,080,000
Factory	----	250,000
NFCU profits		
Fishing	----	144,000
Factory	----	790,000
Traditional craft earnings	630,000	----
TOTAL	630,000	2,264,000

IFI Report

Table 7: Project Employment Estimates

	CURRENT	PROJECTED		
		Fishing	Factory	Total
Skilled	---	80	8	88
Unskilled	420	240	100	340
TOTAL	420	320	108	428

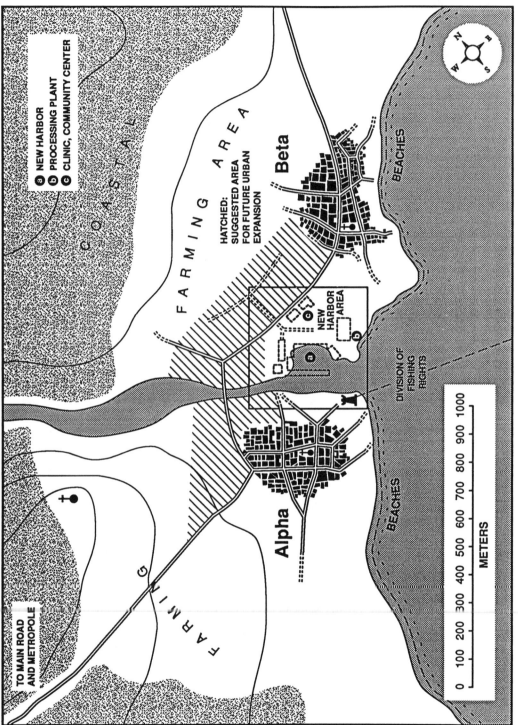

Map of Project Area

"PISCES" CLASS LAUNCH
BARKEXPORT–ODETTA

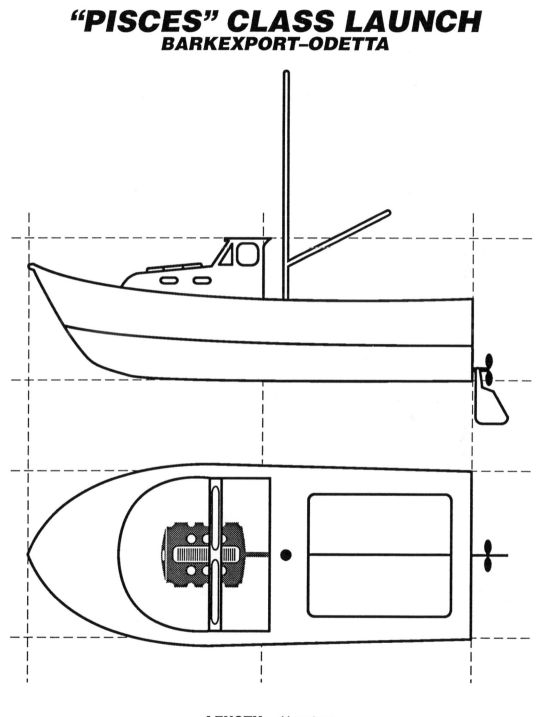

LENGTH:	11 meters
HULL:	fiberglass
ENGINE:	200 hp, diesel inboard engine
SPEED:	12 knots
HOLD CAPACITY:	up to 6 tons
RANGE:	100 km

INSTITUTE OF SOCIAL STUDIES
UNIVERSITY OF METROPOLE

REPORT
TO THE NATIONAL PLANNING COMMISSION
ON THE PROPOSED FISHERIES PROJECT
AT ALPHA-BETA IN KAPPA DISTRICT

INTRODUCTION

Last January the Director of the Institute of Social Studies at Metropole
University was invited by the National Planning Commission to
participate in a feasibility study for a small development project on the
Arcadian coast. It had been proposed that a joint harbor facility should
be provided for two neighboring fishing villages, Alpha and Beta, and
that a plant for freezing fish fillets should be built. The project also
provided for local road improvements and social service facilities in the
form of a new clinic and community center.

The Director of the Institute was delighted to accept this
invitation, welcoming the opportunity to participate in one of the
Government's Special Development Projects and noting that the President
himself had stressed the need to extend the range of considerations which
should be involved in the appraisal of these projects. The Institute was
also pleased to cooperate with the International Fisheries Institute team
investigating the economic aspects of the project and found the brief
collaboration instructive. Dr. Snoop took charge of ISS study in June,
and after several preliminary visits to the area, he conducted a short
survey of Alpha and Beta. In this he was assisted by four research
students from the Institute who lived in the villages for three weeks in
August.

ISS Report

BACKGROUND TO THE PROJECT

The part of the Arcadian coast where the two communities are situated is
renowned for a particularly delicious fish (locally called the goleta)
which is eaten fresh locally and sun-cured for marketing inland. Shoals
of goleta can be found as much as twenty kilometers out to sea, but
fishing operations are currently restricted by the range of local boats to
about three kilometers from the shore. These boats are beached, and are
therefore small, but the growing preference of the more successful
fisherman for outboard motors and larger, stronger nylon nets has led to
local interest in increasing the size and range of the boats. Leaders have
in recent years been petitioning their Legislative Assembly Members and
the District Administration at Kappa (38 km away) for a new harbor
which will provide for the berthing of larger craft.

     The project with which this report is concerned is a response to
these requests. It has been noted that local people have also been
clamoring for a clinic, and it is proposed that this facility should be
incorporated within the project. The needs of the two communities
concerned, Alpha and Beta, are sufficiently similar to enable planners to
design all facilities on the assumption that they will be shared. It is
intended that the road through Alpha and Beta should be improved, and
it has been noted that in a few years the effect of the project as a whole
will probably be to unite the two villages as a single, continuous
settlement. With this in mind, it is proposed that a new clinic /
community center be built mid-way between Alpha and Beta (see map,
IFI Report).

     A general feature of the scheme will be the extension of the
activities of the National Fishermen's Cooperative Union in the two
villages. There have been branches of the NFCU in both communities
for some years, but membership and activities are very limited. The
NFCU has, for example, taken very little interest in the processing and
distribution of sun-dried fish. Under the terms of the project the NFCU
will participate extensively in the organization of the fishing and the
processing of the frozen fillets. These cooperative activities are central
to the attack on poverty in this region. At the moment householders
without boats are dependent on employment on boats operated by other

householders. The intention of the new project is not simply to increase opportunities for wage earning but to bring to the poorest members of the community more direct access to the ownership of productive resources.

BACKGROUND TO THE TWO COMMUNITIES

Although local history is rather vague, it seems clear that Alpha was founded about 200 years ago by the Alpha family and that about 60 years later the Beta family moved out of the village across the river to set up a new settlement now called Beta. The move appears to have been caused by a dispute over fishing rights. Although relationships have been strained from time to time ever since, the dispute was resolved by an agreement that fishing grounds should be divided with reference to a sight line running from the chapel of Santa Maria on a small hill above Alpha to an old watchtower at the river mouth (see map). Within each community, fishing is regulated by an assembly of all the boat-owning householders. These councils adjudicate such matters as who is allowed to beach a boat where, and provide some rudimentary mutual assurance against injury, hardship or loss. They also deal with administrative affairs which do not fall within the purview of the District Council or other bodies, and are officially recognized as "Village Councils" under the provision of the Local Government Act. Leadership of each council is supposedly elective but has been held by direct descendants of Alpha and Beta respectively for as long as anyone can remember. Both villages are almost exclusively Roman Catholic. Each has a small chapel served by a visiting priest responsible for these and two other communities.

The social organization of the two villages is very similar. The settlement pattern is closely nucleated, and buildings vary from five-room brick-built houses with metal roofs to small wood frame, thatched houses, the latter predominating around the seaward side of each community. Each house is quite distinct as a social unit, the household being the principal unit of economic and political organization within the village. The ISS survey enumerated 126 households in Alpha and 117 in Beta. Kinship is reckoned bilaterally, with inheritance of

ISS Report

gardens and "female" property (kitchen utensils, furniture, etc.) passing from mother to daughter, boats and "male" property, including houses, from father to son. Domestic growth may extend to three, occasionally four generations. Family headship is, however, ceded to a son when the father can no longer take an active role in fishing.

Cash income for the villages derives almost entirely from the sale of dried fish inland. Fishing and fish processing activities involve a pronounced division of labor. Boats are owned by households, "mastership" of a boat being a prerogative of the household head. With the present small boats, crews of three or four are the norm. A man without sons or grandsons hires crewmen from other (often boatless) households on a share-catch basis.

Women are allowed nowhere near the boats and are excluded from all fishing activities. They are, however, responsible for cleaning, drying and selling the fish. Fish is sun-cured on racks above the beaches. These racks are constructed of reeds and shared by groups of women, who also have informal partnerships for marketing the fish. In the past, women head-loaded baskets of fish considerable distances, but today much use is made of the numerous privately operated mini-buses which ply throughout Arcadia.

Each household has its own gardens in an area around the town (see map). Women are wholly responsible for these gardens, some of which have quite elaborate systems for dry-season irrigation, drawing water from shallow wells and from the river. The forest behind the villages is mostly in the public domain, and while there is apparently no shortage of land for making new gardens, areas close to each community are at a premium. Only fruit and vegetables are grown locally, and rice, the main staple, is bought from outside the area.

SOCIOLOGICAL PROBLEMS PRESENTED BY THE PROJECT

Set against this outline of community organization, the proposed project raises a number of sociological questions. In the following sections we consider the most salient of these in the light of the ISS survey data, and suggest ways in which our findings may be brought to bear on the evaluation of the project.

Firstly we shall specify the economic, political and social changes which are either intended or implicit in the basic plan:

(a) A new technical base will be established, with a view to alleviating poverty and providing the means for further economic and social development. Methods for catching, processing, and marketing of fish will all be radically changed.

(b) The most notable changes in economic organization will be a shift towards wage earning, extension of principles of formal cooperative organization and multiplication of opportunities for private enterprise.

(c) Working relationships among men and among women (in boat and factory) will be restructured. This will have pervasive consequences for the domestic and public relationships between the sexes and between generations.

(d) New patterns of earning and improved access to capital and markets will change the existing pattern of socio-economic differentiation, and the disposition of political authority.

(e) Local economic opportunities will attract outsiders, thereby altering the social and political composition of the communities.

(f) A process will be initiated by which the two communities will develop into a single economic, political and social unit.

(g) The locality will become more closely integrated with the wider region and the nation, confronting local people with new opportunities and constraints.

In an attempt to elucidate these issues, a brief survey of the two villages was carried out by the ISS team. It was decided to collect a limited amount of information from all economically active persons (hereafter simply described as "adults") in the two villages, rather than attempting to conduct a more detailed sample survey. It was felt that this would provide up-to-date census material for the project, and an accurate basis for the canvassing of attitudes. It should be noted that

ISS Report

outline plans for the project had been discussed at public meetings in both villages and that our survey established, on the basis of a checklist, that virtually all adults knew something of plans for the proposed harbor, boats, factory, road improvements, clinic and community center.

In the light of the main sociological issues raised by the project, we have arranged the ISS data, for the purposes of this report, in terms of the categories listed in the table below. To discover who is in favor of the proposed project and who is not, we asked this direct question:

"Do you think that, all things considered, you will be better off when the new project is established than you are now?"

	Number	Percentage of positive responses
Total population of both villages	1716	
Total adult population of Alpha	460	58
Total adult population of Beta	433	79
Total adult population of both villages	893	68
Heads of households dependent on fishing	206	59
Heads of households dependent on other activities (e.g. shopkeepers)	37	62
Total households	243	
Fishing household heads owning no boats	68	87
Fishing household heads owning one or more boats	138	56
Adult men of both villages	450	61
Adult women of both villages	443	77
Total adult population aged under 45	750	72
Total adult population aged over 45	143	55

ISS Report

From this table we can see that within the overall majority favorably disposed to the basic project, there are considerable variations in opinion. Beta adults are more positively disposed than Alpha adults, women more than men, and younger people more than older people. It is also apparent that household heads who do not own boats are more optimistic about the scheme than those who do own boats. We may tentatively conclude that the project is likely to meet less opposition from the younger and poorer mass of the community than from the older men who are household heads, especially those who own boats. However, it is clearly this second category which currently wields the greatest influence in community affairs and is likely to be a force to be reckoned with.

As a general indication of opinion in the two villages the above figures are helpful, but further elucidation by direct and indirect testing was clearly required in the survey.

RESULTS OF THE SOCIOLOGICAL ANALYSIS

(a) Technical and Economic Change
The survey makes it evident that technical innovations, infrastructural facilities and planned amenities are less likely to cause local resistance than matters of boat ownership, the organization of labor and marketing, and the siting of the new facilities.

Three-quarters of the adult males agreed that bigger boats were desirable, but many of them foresaw difficulties in terms of ownership and new crewing arrangements. The survey asked them to state the disadvantages of larger boats. Many complained of the high capital cost which would make it difficult for an individual to acquire a controlling interest in the boat. A change in skippering and crewing arrangements would cause disputes, and competition from the bigger boats would be unfair to owners of the remaining smaller boats. Although the problem of managing fish stocks had been explained at public meetings, it was still generally assumed that a substantial number of smaller boats could continue to operate alongside the new launches. The small boats have

ISS Report

functions (river communications, shellfish collection) which the bigger boats could not perform. The existing boats are usually objects of family pride, and there may be strong sentimental obstacles to replacing them. Controlling the activities of the older boats which remain will certainly pose problems.

Householders who owned no boats, and those with poorer craft, tended to feel that "more people should share in the ownership of bigger boats." However, 67 per cent of all heads of fishing households felt that eventually ownership of the new launches would and should pass into the control of individual households; only 28 per cent thought that they should remain in cooperative ownership through the NFCU.

The largest proportion of adult men (61 per cent) felt that household heads should lead the crew of the new boats, and only 9 per cent felt it was appropriate that they should be skippered by seamen from outside the two villages. Forty per cent would be happy to see a trained local man who was not a household head placed in charge of a boat.

In matters of ownership and operation there was a great deal of mistrust about the future role of the NFCU, particularly in Beta, where the chairman, one of the wealthiest household heads, was recently implicated in the collapse of a scheme to purchase nylon nets. Currently, only 33 per cent of the adult men in Alpha, and 21 per cent in Beta, are NFCU members. Younger men seemed to take a favorable view of opportunities to acquire shares in the new boats (understanding of such possibilities was vague) and were enthusiastic about the prospect of working for wages. Older men tended to point out that without the inducement of the present share-catch system the younger generation would show little interest in hard work. In general, it was the very poorest and the very richest household heads who were most enthusiastic about NFCU control of fishing. For the former there was the hope of an immediate increase in income, and for the latter there was the attraction of being able to acquire a controlling interest in one or more boats, if not control over the whole NFCU operation.

The reorganization of processing principally concerns the women of the two villages who, it is hoped, will supply most of the labor for the new factory. Rumors of high wages have made a majority of women very optimistic: 64 per cent of the adult women said that they will

ISS Report

probably seek work in the factory. Nearly all the women from boatless households (91 per cent) said that they would seek factory work. Although no questions were specifically asked about women's present role in curing and marketing fish, it was apparent that many assumed that these activities would continue alongside factory employment. A substantial 33 per cent of adult men said that they would disapprove of a woman member of their household working in the factory, the usual reason being that this would distract them from their domestic responsibilities. Many men, however, shrugged off the question, saying that it was the business of the women to make up their own minds.

The women were generally unenthusiastic about NFCU membership and about NFCU control of fish marketing. Fifty-four per cent of them disapproved of this monopoly, complaining that it would disrupt long-established trading arrangements, many aspects of which they valued. Questions about marketing evoked relatively little interest among the men, who tended to tell the interviewers "you must ask my wife about that."

In general, it seems that women are quite well disposed towards their proposed role in the project, but it is clear that their participation will bring far-reaching changes to domestic organization. Presumably, horticulture will decline sharply, and some alternative arrangements will have to be made in many cases for the care of children. It is likely that factory employment will leave women with little time or inclination for continuing their present role in curing and marketing, and in any case virtually all the catch will be diverted to the factory. In sum, we would guess that the women are more likely to adjust to rapid change than the men, even if the effects of rapid change will disrupt their domestic life to a greater extent in the long run.

(b) Political Implications.

The success of the proposed scheme clearly depends on close cooperation between the two villages, in the immediate future and in the long term. Given the existing rivalry between the two communities it may be foreseen that the project will inevitably be affected by factionalism in its early stages. The location of the new facilities is already a source of contention, going some way to accounting for the more positive attitude

ISS Report

of the people of Beta to the basic plan. The people of Alpha often asked interviewers why it was not possible for them to have their own harbor and factory and complained that the proposed location of the clinic and community center was too much in favor of Beta. Only 61 per cent of the Alpha adults thought that the proposed location of the harbor was a sensible choice (from a technical point of view it is the only choice). While 88 per cent of the Beta people approved of the site of the clinic and community center, only 31 per cent of the Alpha people thought this reasonable. They often pointed out that the indirect gains to the Beta people, particularly in land transactions and opportunities to start new service businesses, would be much greater. However, it was notable that roughly half of the population of both villages (47 per cent in Alpha, 55 per cent in Beta) regarded the long-term development of the two villages into a single "town" favorably. It was generally agreed that the division of fishing rights should disappear, but the chairman of the Alpha village council pointed out that the customary legal complexities of this were such that any change would necessarily involve lengthy negotiations.

It seems that this political division will affect most seriously the participation of local people in the management of the project - elections and appointments to the local NFCU branch, routine processes of decision making while the project is under way and so on. While the safest strategy may be to exclude local people from the management of the scheme in its early stages, this carries the risk of further diminishing local enthusiasm for the project and for NFCU activities. Once the economic activities of the two villages are firmly under a single management structure, it is likely that the social and political divisions between them will rapidly diminish in significance. It is possible that a more positive attitude to the project in Alpha could be bought by redistributing the proposed amenities more in their favor. Such an approach could be costly and technically difficult. It is tempting to argue that if the facilities are presented to the people as a fait accompli they will eventually accept them, but if they are invited to discuss the location of amenities this will only exacerbate the division of interest between the two villages.

ISS Report

(c) The Distribution of Benefits

A survey of the kind conducted cannot hope to throw very much light on one of the most important questions: "Who stands to gain most from the implementation of this project?" The Planning Commission will not need to be reminded of our President's concern for the eradication of poverty and the creation of new economic opportunities. The general guidelines for this are laid down in The Common People's Charter, and epitomized in our Government's watchword: "All Arcadia for All Arcadians." In these terms, the apparent enthusiasm of the poorer people of Alpha and Beta for the proposed project is a good omen. Likewise, youth is on the side of the project, suggesting that in the fullness of time the scheme will prosper. The National Council for Women will undoubtedly welcome the new opportunities which are being provided as enthusiastically as the women of the two villages themselves. In short, the basic project seems very much in tune with the social welfare policies of Arcadia.

It is apparent that household heads are apprehensive about their control of fishing and community affairs. They will not easily relinquish their authority, and inevitably it is with them that Government personnel will have to deal, at least in the initial stages of the project. We were told that the wealthiest households are already buying up plots of land around the river mouth and seeking licenses to run garage, retailing and other businesses. The 37 non-fishing household heads are divided in their opinions about how they will fare under the scheme; some clearly look forward to expanding their retail and service businesses, but others, particularly older women traders with a very small turnover, felt that their livelihood is threatened. Few local people seem to think that an invasion of outsiders was likely, but when the question was put to them: "Do you think that people from outside Alpha and Beta should be given jobs on the new boats and in the new factory?" only 11 per cent answered affirmatively.

ISS Report

PROJECT IMPLEMENTATION

On the basis of observed need and the expressed opinions of the people themselves, the ISS survey leaves little doubt that the Alpha-Beta Fisheries Development Project should be implemented. However diverse the attitudes of the local people (there are, after all, divergences of interest in all communities), if the crude choice was between having a development project and not having one, the verdict would surely be unanimously in favor.

The essential challenge for the Planning Commission, therefore, is how to put the project into effect while minimizing social and political constraints and building on local institutions and initiatives. A conspicuous social consideration is the speed with which the new technical and economic systems are implanted in the two communities. From an economic perspective, the sooner the new boats and factory are functioning, the better. It could be said that the enthusiasm of the local people is ultimately dependent on the size of the material rewards offered and how soon these rewards appear. Rapid implementation might have the effect of reducing opposition to the project, but a more gradual introduction of the new technology would allow time for adaptation and for peaceful resolution of incipient conflicts.

However, this more gradual approach would in turn require a more intensive, socially aware form of management, a new social contract between administrators and local people of the sort which both the Government of Arcadia and the Institute of Social Studies would seek to encourage.

A.Snoop, M.A., PhD.
Professor of Sociology
Institute of Social Studies
University of Metropole
Metropole 10371
Arcadia

ISS Report

Rick Rinegold
& Bobby Lee

DISCOVERING
ARCADIA

WP

9

Fisherfolk

Maria was one of the most captivating characters in the marketplace. Sitting among her pungent wares, she scolded us fiercely for refusing to buy. Seeing us squirm, she threw her head back, closed her twinkling eyes, and hooted with mirth. Among so many brightly clad Theta women, Maria was conspicuous not for her appearance—her slight frame was shrouded in drab blues and browns—but for her voice and manner. The other women made little pyramids of brilliant red and yellow tomatoes, tied spinach leaves into lustrous bunches, measured snowy mounds of rice into brown paper cones, and chatted amiably with their customers. Maria's restless fingers turned the leathery fish in the baskets around her, and as if to compensate for its uninviting appearance, she yelled its virtues at the crowd.

Here, she cried, holding up a wrinkled sample, was goleta, queen of the ocean; caught by brave men, dried in the shimmering sun, and carried by strong women to the lucky folk of this landlocked town. Even *you*—her extended forefinger stopped a passing matron in her tracks—could release the succulent flavor of this fish in a tasty stew. Yes, even you could reawaken the weary palate of your disgruntled husband and worm your way down to his heart and loins.

Truly, these people needed little persuasion. Already the odors that curled around the marketplace had tickled their nostrils and moistened their lips. They stooped noncommittally over Maria's baskets, fingers itching to palpate the firm flesh of the fish. They were already trapped in her volley of insults and jests, and each customer knew to her chagrin that her own discomfiture was already driving the price up a cent or two.

Our friends in Theta clicked their tongues disapprovingly but would never admit that they were intimidated. *These fisherfolk are not like us. Listen to that rude voice, those coarse manners! Of course, despite appearances, they are all rich. Did you see how much we had to pay for one shriveled piece of fish? It's not as if they had to grow these things, the way we farmers have to struggle to raise our crops and rear our animals. These people haul fish by the thousand out of the sea and then bring us the rubbish they cannot eat themselves.* We did not try to persuade them that Maria's strident voice was the spirited challenge of a people whose lives are hard and perilous and who must oblige the wider world to compensate them for their struggle.

For a few minutes, we distract Maria from her pitch to take a photograph, a bargaining process as intense as if we had been bidding for a kilo or two of goleta.

We ask her about her home, which must be more than a day's journey from here. Alpha, she tells us, is on a strip of beach where the Kappa River dribbles out into the ocean like an old man's piss. It's at the end of the world, a village where the gnats rule the cockroaches. Ah, but down there, the men are men, and the women are women, and we give thanks to God for His bounty from the deep. After He divided night from day, did He not then divide heaven from the waters that were below the firmament? And then—her work-stained fingers fasten on our clothes—did He not *finally* get around to gathering up the waters to let the dry land appear? Places like *this*—she waves disparagingly at the ramshackle houses of Theta. So why the devil should we care where she comes from?

We tell her rather grandly that we are discovering Arcadia and are perplexed by her helpless laughter. She wipes her eyes and pats our hands placatingly. Come to Alpha, she says, and discover us. We will feed you and make you happy.

✦ ✦ ✦

We drive to Alpha one Saturday morning, turning seaward at the point where the Kappa River crosses the coast road. We thread our way through the low, forested hills so characteristic of this part of the Arcadian coast. We admire its tropical foliage, shallow marshlands, and estuaries, but we know that this land is not as hospitable as it appears. The evening air will whine with a myriad tiny wings. Anyone mad enough to linger by an exquisite moonlit lagoon will be bled dry.

The communities of Alpha and Beta confront each other across the turgid waters of the river. At this final stage of its journey from the interior, it is less than two hundred feet wide. It is spanned by a narrow bridge standing on uncertain piles, stained by the rise and fall of the tide.

As the road emerges from the forest, our map tells us that the slender spire on the hillside to our left is the chapel of Saint Mary, site of an early missionary enclave on this coast. We thread our way toward Alpha through what seems to be a single enormous backyard of vegetable plots and garbage heaps. The road deposits us in the narrow streets of Alpha, and we press on through curious stares. Walls close in around us, and just when we feel that the car will be jammed fast, we find ourselves on the shoreline.

What did we expect? Umbrellas, Pepsi vendors, bikinis and sailboards, bronzed flesh reeking of suntan oil? This is not the seaside as tourists would imagine it. We behold a tableau from the past, its colors and sounds fixed in our memories by that pervasive fragrance to which Maria had introduced us. Between the beach and the clustered houses stand broad racks laden with the famous goleta, scorching in the sun. Repeatedly softened and seasoned with saltwater, the fish ripen, and their odor permeates the air that drifts lazily over the beach and through the town. The shores of this community are still dominated by its traditional industry, and they will have to suffer more than a sea change before they can accommodate the fastidious feet of the vacationer. Yet today this narrow strip of sand seems busier than Copacabana or Bondi: seething with activity and serving the functions of harbor, boatyard, factory, marketplace, refuse dump, playground, and latrine. . .

✦ ✦ ✦

Alpha is a cluster of brick and wood frame houses, home to perhaps a thousand souls. It faces inward, both to its own narrow streets and to the hills beyond. It is as if these people were weary of the ocean, turning their backs on its vastness and uncertainty. The community seems to yearn for an affiliation with the land and for the intimacy of close neighborhood. On the inland side there are scattered signs of modernity: a gas station with two battered pumps and a vast refrigerator, a soccer pitch dominated by four floodlight gantries, and an assortment of advertisement hoardings. The wealthier denizens have gravitated to this landward side, building courtyards of brick and concrete. Nearer the sea the poverty for which this region is well known makes itself painfully evident: Rickety dwellings of mud and thatch huddle behind the bigger houses; women nursing tiny children squat on the earth by open hearths; ragged boys and girls fetch water in plastic buckets from faucets in more privileged streets.

By contrast, the boats make a merry spectacle. In the evening they are drawn up under the palms, a parade of brightly painted prows. Their flanks are decorated with strange, superstitious signs—an eye, a coiled serpent, a radiant sun. In varying sizes and states of repair, they conform to a basic design: square stern for casting nets, broad beam for the catch, and a tall bow for breasting the waves. We can see this scheme most clearly in the white bones of a new boat up on stocks in the shade of the palm trees.

We seek shelter there from the afternoon sun to watch the busy scene. At this hour the boats are returning home through the surf, some with their bellies full of glittering fish. Brawny shoulders bend to the oars, drawing their cargo against the tide. Two men pull from the center of the boat, and a third—surely the paterfamilias, with cap and pipe—steadies the craft with the rudder oar.

Sea and land, men and women converge on that mysterious threshold that is the shore. The women spread mats beside each boat at the water's edge, count and divide the catch, gut the fish, and toss them into baskets. This is done amid much clamor, the voices of men and women raised in argument as the fish are moved from here to there. Above their heads the brazen gulls scream and thrash the air. Relays of men haul the emptied boats over the sand, a marvel of concerted effort. Now boards have to be sluiced, nets spread out and cleaned, lines coiled, and oars stowed.

We are so absorbed in this scene that we have not noticed the lengthening shadows. While adults gravitate into the village, the children take possession of the beach. Small boys turn like dolphins in the breaking surf, taunting their sisters who watch them demurely from the sand.

We make our way back into the narrow streets of the town and find their mothers as busy as ever: washing and setting out the fish, preparing the family supper, heading for their gardens with hoes over their shoulders. In the morning they had charge of these streets, but the men have taken possession once again. They sit together in doorways or on benches under the shade trees, cutting the heavy air with voices they have honed at sea, calling from boat to boat.

Like Maria's inland customers, we are on our guard as we approach the tavern door, unsure of our welcome. Quicker than we might wish we are drawn in by coarse, friendly hands and settled on benches. Glasses of pale liquor are set before us. We are informed that it is brewed "somewhere over there" (vague gesture to the seaward side of the town) and is known as "shuttle" after the American space vehicle. We note that one or two topers around us have already entered the stratosphere. One of us sips and the other swigs, but the wicked fluid scorches both of us on its way down to our bellies. After a moment's suspense its vapors sweep up and smack the inside of our skulls.

We are quizzed very directly about our business. With little confidence we try again to explain our mission to discover Arcadia. Once again, broad grins and guffaws. Somewhat piqued, we try to match their candor: What is so ridiculous about our curiosity?

Voice chimes upon voice in rough-hewn poetry. We are people who live where the land is swallowed up by the ocean. We are the wretched of the earth, beaten back to the shoreline, drawing slivers of living silver from the black depths. We have driven stakes for our boats into this narrow space between hill and wave. The only certainty we face is death, and even then no man knows whether he will be consumed by worms or by fishes. Here on the edge of the world—stubby fingers smack the corner of a table—we have dominion over nothing. It is the business of other people to have dominion over us.

Then after these verses, a characteristic change of tune: What do *we* think of the words of this particular government minister? How just is the new tax on alcohol? Will America send its soldiers over there to keep peace in that country? Why did so many people die when the storm struck this other country? Of course they had answers of their own. Newspapers, television, and the radio especially are no strangers in this town, and in their ceaseless conversations the people construct and reconstruct the wider world. What amused them about us was a turning of the tables: the notion that people from Metropole should express an interest in *them*.

So we insist: How should we describe them to the wider world?

The gravity of the question affects them, and we are led in solemn procession through the streets to the back (or is it the front?) of the town, to the house of the shrewd octogenarian who is the father of this ramifying family. On a second-story veranda touched by the low sunlight, we are told something of the history of this place and much about the agony of daily life on the margins of the ocean.

Once again we are struck by the rhetoric of these simple folk: vivid, allusive, with many words spoken and few wasted. As we sit in our wicker chairs listening to this authoritative tale, we are graciously and without invitation entertained to supper. The fruits of the sea are spread before us: fresh crab, tiny rock fish, and of course the famous goleta—not in the pungent form we had discovered inland but freshly grilled. For our expectant hosts, we could readily rhapsodize about its texture and flavor—juicy and firm, evocative of croaker we had tasted on the Louisiana coast. We ate our fill shamelessly, balking only at a sour sauce of fermented fish that is a specialty of the region and very certainly an acquired taste.

✦　✦　✦

In Alpha we never found our friend Maria.

Everyone shrugged. Maria who? We have a thousand Marias here, and those who are not bearing our children or turning the fish on the drying racks are out there somewhere in the night, traveling with their baskets to some distant corner of Arcadia.

PART TWO: PROPOSALS

NATIONAL PLANNING COMMISSION
GOVERNMENT OF THE REPUBLIC OF ARCADIA

12 Avenue of the Republic
Metropole 10001
Arcadia

"Helping People to
Help Themselves"

Tel: 201-3333

Fax: 201-3344

REGIONAL PROJECTS DIVISION
SPECIAL PROJECTS ADVISORY COMMITTEE

Agenda for meeting - July 14

FISHERIES DEVELOPMENT PROJECT FOR ALPHA AND BETA

Following intensive discussion at the meeting of the Special Projects Advisory
Committee on May 21 last, it was decided to postpone approval of the
proposed Fisheries Project in the villages of Alpha and Beta until alternative
implementation plans had been more carefully considered. Accordingly, it was
agreed that the Committee would resolve itself into four working groups,
based on differences of opinion manifest during the meeting. Each group
would table a proposal for consideration at the plenary session on July 14 next.

It is within the powers of the SPAC to recommend that the project be
abandoned as unfeasible at this stage. Accordingly, it is suggested that
proposals for implementation should proceed from a brief appraisal of the
viability of the basic specifications of the project.

As Chair of the Special Projects Advisory Committee, I propose the following
guidelines for drafting these proposals:

Evaluation:

- Is the project economically, technically, and socially feasible?
  - Does it promise sound returns to investment of national and local resources?
  - Does it make efficient but ecologically responsible use of available resources?

- Is the project in accordance with the Government's commitment to eliminate poverty and distribute widely the benefits of development?
  - Does it improve the economic, social and political status of women?
  - Does it benefit members of the community not directly involved in the catching and processing of fish?

Implementation:

Bearing in mind these criteria, proposals for implementing the project should attend to the following special requirements:

- The managerial role of the Fishermen's Cooperative:
  In view of the particular responsibilities of the NFCU in this project, implementation guidelines should specify such matters as control and operation of processing plant and new craft, crewing arrangements, selection and training of operatives, structure of rewards, shareholding, &c.

- Scheduling:
  Given that the project must be fully operational within four years of installation of the basic infrastructure, proposals should specify how and when the main components of the project should be implemented. For example, phasing-in of new craft and removal of old craft, selection and training of fishing crews, factory operatives, &c.

- Replicability:
  In addition to maximizing the benefits of the project locally and nationally, and securing the compliance and cooperation of the

people of Alpha and Beta, implementation plans should lend themselves to transfer to other coastal regions of Arcadia.

In clarification of one issue arising at the May 21 meeting: budgetary provisions for this project are as specified and cannot be expanded arbitrarily to accommodate more costly implementation proposals. Nor are alterations to the basic infrastructure and technical provisions (harbor structures, vessel type, &c.) admissable at this stage. If the Special Projects Advisory Committee finds these basic terms and conditions unacceptable, it may recommend that the project be halted and referred back to the Planning Commission for redrafting. It should of course be noted, however, that this would add considerably to the overall cost of the project.

Zero Sifer
Director, Regional Projects Division

NATIONAL PLANNING COMMISSION
GOVERNMENT OF THE REPUBLIC OF ARCADIA

12 Avenue of the Republic
Metropole 10001
Arcadia

"Helping People to
Help Themselves"

Tel: 201-3333

Fax: 201-3344

REGIONAL PROJECTS DIVISION
SPECIAL PROJECTS ADVISORY COMMITTEE

Documents for meeting - July 14

FISHERIES DEVELOPMENT PROJECT FOR ALPHA AND BETA

I attach hereto copies of the proposals I have received from the four subgroups of the Special Projects Advisory Committee, concerning the implementation of the Fisheries Development Project for the villages of Alpha and Beta in Kappa District.

The Committee will convene at 9:00 a.m. prompt on July 14 to discuss these proposals, and draft a recommendation to the National Planning Commission.

Zero Sifer
Director, Regional Projects Division

SPECIAL PROJECTS ADVISORY COMMITTEE: THE ALPHA-BETA FISHERIES PROJECT

EVALUATION AND IMPLEMENTATION PROPOSAL BY GROUP A

At a two-hour meeting on June 2 last, Group A of the Special Projects Advisory Committee agreed unanimously to advise immediate implementation of this coastal development plan.

1.   EVALUATION

The group was impressed by the Planning Commission's foresight in developing this project, and the skill with which the International Fisheries Institute has drawn up the basic specification. The IFI's summary report (section 6) itself offers a positive appraisal of the project, justifying its efficiency, income-generating prospects, multiplier effects, and wider social benefits. The basic proposal is imaginative yet straightforward - indeed, it would be hard to think of a more appropriate development program for this area. It responds to the expressed needs of the local people, builds on their skills and capacities, and exploits a natural resource for the benefit of producers and consumers alike in an ecologically responsible way.

　　　　With an estimated internal rate of return in the order of 12%, the project is an effective model for change. It challenges the local people to work for progress and will go far to redress the balance between this notably poor region and other parts of Arcadia. The infrastructure package is remarkably generous, and the capital contribution which the people of Alpha and Beta are being asked to make is relatively modest. The "Pisces" class fishing boats are a very good bargain. The relatively high manning levels proposed for the new boats and the intensity of labor use in the factory, are enlightened responses to the need to preserve high levels of employment and broad distribution of incomes.

　　　　In sum, it would be a grave dereliction of our public responsibility *not* to endorse this plan and advocate its speedy implementation.

*SPAC - **GROUP A***

2.   "DYNAMIC, DECISIVE DEVELOPMENT"

Group A strongly urges that this initiative be pursued expeditiously, in accordance with our government's commitment to "Dynamic, Decisive Development" - the watchword of our current National Five-Year Plan.

The most serious threat to the project would be well-intentioned efforts to protract and complicate what already is a simple and coherent basic plan. The sooner the new facilities are in place and functioning, the earlier the material rewards can be reaped. Time is money, and money will be our greatest asset in dealing with the inevitable teething troubles of a project.

It is accordingly recommended that all the new boats and the factory be scheduled for full operation immediately after completion of the basic infrastructure (harbor, roads, &c.). Slowing down the installation of the new fleet will erode the profitability of the enterprise, multiply managerial and transaction costs, confuse the local people, and set precedents for the inefficient use of scarce capital resources.

3.   INSTALLING THE NEW FLEET

Under any circumstances, the elimination of the old boats must be the most painful part of the project. However, to make an omelette, eggs must be broken. The sociology report notes that although the people fear the competition of new boats, they also want the project to proceed. This is an understandably equivocal attitude to change - an ambivalent concern for both security and progress. It is natural that they should find it hard to see the connection between the need to use better boats to get bigger catches and the need to protect fish stocks by eliminating such a highly valued capital asset, the old boats.

Every effort should be made to characterize the new boats as a direct substitute for the old. The problem should be dealt with emphatically and conclusively. It is suggested that the inauguration of the new boats should be celebrated fiesta-style, culminating in the ceremonial burning of the old boats. This should be conducted, with full media attention and with the endorsement of the church, as an act of propitiation for the new way of life. Should such a dramatic measure be considered inappropriate or impractical, then economic

*SPAC - **GROUP A***

forces will themselves solve the problem: the new fleet will rapidly put the old out of business by fishing-out the shallower water after the breeding season.

Group A can see no virtue in attempting to mix the old and the new modes of fishing and is confident that the people will quickly perceive the material advantages of embracing the new system. As sociologists never tire of telling us, it is the stranglehold of poverty, not a lack of imagination, which causes backwardness. The forces of "tradition" are greatly overrated as an obstacle to modernization. We presume that the people of Alpha and Beta are as rational in their perception of real opportunities as any of us. Their use of such technical advances as outboard motors indicates that they are already accustomed to responding to new opportunities.

4.   TECHNICAL INITIATIVES FOR SOCIAL CHANGE

The project management should therefore encourage active participation by accentuating the profitability of the new fishing and processing operations from the beginning. Forty new deep-sea vessels pose something of a revolution, but if these fishermen show any reluctance to get involved, it will only be because they lack coherent information and convincing evidence that the new technology works. A catch some seventeen times greater than the average for the old boats and some thirty-two times more profitable will rapidly and convincingly demonstrate the virtues of the new system. By the same token, any implementation measures which detract from this demonstration will diminish the incentives to participate.

The project should build on the driving force of technical change, a process which has already taken root in this and every other community in Arcadia. The question is not whether Alpha and Beta will be transformed, but *when*. It is futile, even dangerous, to anticipate in any detail how the communities will react, and unnecessarily patronizing to try to engineer an elaborate social structure in order to mitigate the inevitable pains of adjustment. It is better to press ahead with the practical tasks than to engage in pointless speculation about whether, for example, political factions in Alpha and Beta will cripple the project. Given the pressure on public budgets, it would be unconscionable for management to supply the time or the opportunity for any of the supposed beneficiaries of this

*SPAC - **GROUP A***

project to create spurious obstacles.

The momentum of these considerable technical and organizational changes will initiate rapid demographic growth and coalescence of the two villages into a single small urban zone, submerging the petty divisions of interests which are evidently a constraint on progress today. The disconcerted voices of Alpha and Beta are simply crying out for authoritative leadership, which the management of this project can and should provide.

5.   COOPERATION AND ENTREPRENEURSHIP IN PROJECT MANAGEMENT

The approach recommended by Group A is predicated on strong management. The longer-term intention, however, is to ensure that the individual participants have the fullest opportunity to reap the benefits of the project. The basic plan leans heavily on their "obligation to cooperate" through the medium of the NFCU. While this may seem the obvious choice, it could also prove to be the weakest link in the development process. While every effort must be made to enhance the efficiency of the local branch, there is no reason to suppose that it will be able to turn these two villages into a little socialist Utopia. Experience with cooperatives in this and other countries has shown that they work best when short- and medium-term targets are clearly set and when individual participants have a strong perception of how these goals serve the interests of themselves and their immediate families.

In this case the central goal should be private ownership of capital - the boats and the factory - through the medium of shareholding in a corporate enterprise. In other words, it is entirely appropriate to expect that the NFCU will not remain in control in perpetuity but serve as a bridge to the establishment of an Alpha-Beta Fisheries Corporation, akin to similar privately owned businesses throughout the country.

For the foreseeable future, it seems important to regard fleet and factory as an interdependent entity, since the one cannot function adequately without the services of the other. Likewise, it seems unwise to allow the new boats to devolve into private, competitive ownership, at least until the ten-year amortization period is over.

While healthy private enterprise should be the goal, there is a proper expectation that the project will be established on the basis of full equality of opportunity. At the outset, every adult citizen of Alpha and Beta, without distinction of sex, who finds employment on either the boats or in the factory will have the right to full vote-bearing membership in the Fishermen's Cooperative. Recruitment will be on a voluntary first-come, first-served basis: the boats and the factory will be staffed first, and late recruits will be accommodated as soon as the Cooperative can generate subsidiary enterprises, as described below. Initially, wages will remain as prescribed in the basic plan but may be adjusted by the NFC as patterns of profit are reassessed annually.

Co-op membership will constitute a capital share in the enterprise, which will accumulate in value during the life of the project. At a stage no earlier than the fifth year of the project, these shares, with their attendant votes in the NFC, will become transferable. In effect, a market in project participation and capital acquisition will be initiated. At this stage the project will become anchored securely in private entrepreneurial interest and in the freedom to choose whether or not to participate. From then on, shareholders can decide on a ballot of members whether project management should remain within the NFCU or should be constituted as an autonomous corporation under the terms of the Companies Act.

In the first five years the NFCU will have ample opportunity to prove itself as an efficient manager of the project and to benefit accordingly. An annual budget of A.300,000, written into the administrative costs of the factory, makes very generous provision for the recruitment of a tough and experienced management team, on which successful installation of the project will depend.

The certified seamen and the technical / supervisory staff of the factory will also be recruited from outside the area and placed on two-year renewable contracts. Through the agency of the Cooperative, they will be replaced by local people, suitably trained on the job. This will provide some promotion incentives within the enterprise as it develops.

6. SUBSIDIARY INVESTMENT PROGRAM

From the substantial profits generated by the enterprise, the Cooperative will initiate a scheme of loans, subsidies and incentives to establish ancillary businesses for the benefit of those who are not incorporated into the labor force of the fleet and factory. The NFC will favor small businesses like chandlery, mechanical repair, cafeteria,

*SPAC - **GROUP A***

child care, and other establishments which directly service the fishing industry.

By fostering private enterprise in this way, the project can acquit its obligation to those who are members of the community but have not become, for whatever reason, shareholders in the Cooperative. The sociological report notes that those not currently involved in fishing are rather more positively disposed towards the project, which suggests that ancillary developments of the kind envisaged here will be welcomed.

7.   DISTRIBUTION OF PROJECT BENEFITS

It will be evident that this proposal treats men and women equally with regard to participation in both the immediate and long-term benefits of the project. Indeed, women may well be placed at some advantage, since it appears that they are already experienced small-scale entrepreneurs, trading in dried fish over considerable.distances. On the other hand, shareholding principles should come quite naturally to the fishermen, who are accustomed to share-catch arrangements. It may be assumed that the demands of crewing small boats at sea will have equipped them with basic cooperative skills.

There is no reason why benefits from national investment in these two communities should remain confined within these two villages. Investment of public resources carries social responsibilities to all Arcadians, and after the initial period of protection nothing should be done to restrict either the trickle-down or the trickle-out effects. Thus, after five years the market for shares in the project should not discriminate between community members and outsiders.

8.   "HELPING PEOPLE TO HELP THEMSELVES"

The benefits of the businesslike approach to implementation advocated here are many. There is every reason to suppose that the project is dealing with skillful, rational, self-interested people, who will quickly perceive the virtues of active commitment to the enterprise. Special Projects strike a bargain with the people to collaborate in their own interests with government agencies. While clear and authoritative management will be essential in the initial stages, no measures should be taken which will thwart the development of a healthy, competitive, entrepreneurial spirit. Only this wholehearted, self-interested involvement will generate the wealth which will redeem

*SPAC - **GROUP A***

this region from its current poverty.

The intention is very plainly to draw Alpha-Beta into the mainstream of Arcadian life and to bring to this impoverished area some of the benefits of involvement in the wider world. This - as any businessman knows - will also entail costs, which the people themselves will have to confront. The lesson of modern history is that any pretense on the part of government to turn these villages into Utopia-by-the-Sea is a cruel fraud.

An implementation plan which builds on the entrepreneurial zeal of the people and cuts bureaucratic clutter to a minimum will be more easily transferable to other coastal regions of Arcadia. The government is offering a substantial gift of development and should feel no obligation to bully or cajole these people into compliance. The best recipe for success is to put the infrastructure and capital into place as rapidly as possible and insist that the people themselves take their destiny into their own hands.

Nothing could be more in keeping with the government's commitment, so clearly articulated in the Common People's Charter, to "Help People to Help Themselves."

*SPAC - **GROUP A***

SPECIAL PROJECTS ADVISORY COMMITTEE: THE ALPHA-BETA FISHERIES PROJECT

EVALUATION AND IMPLEMENTATION PROPOSAL BY GROUP B

INTRODUCTION

We believe the basic project is sound and timely. A development program in such a poor area is, in all conscience, essential. The new technology is a logical advance on local fishing and fish processing. If firm measures are taken to establish efficient cooperative management, there are good prospects that the benefits will be distributed equitably. The Institute of Social Studies report tells us that the underdogs -- the poorer people, youth, and women -- are most enthusiastic about the development plan. We must ensure that management will serve their interests fully and effectively, because without their wholehearted participation the project will surely collapse.

We are convinced that it will be both necessary and in the long run advantageous to implement the plan *gradually*. We would argue that the project will, under any circumstances, have to be phased in: it is simply unrealistic to assume that all the new boats will be available and functioning on the first day of the project, and that the factory will be able to cope immediately with 10,000 tons of fish. It is impossible to imagine that 140 traditional fishing boats, treasured family possessions, can be removed overnight to make way for the new boats -- especially as 100 men would immediately be put out of work. Any attempt to do this would require some sort of violence and would generate anger and confusion which would be to the detriment of the project in the long term.

Rather than having to keep reorganizing and rescheduling to cope with such problems, let us anticipate them at the outset. We therefore propose that the project budget should be adjusted to *buy time* to

*SPAC - **GROUP B***

allow both the project management and the people to adapt to the inevitable problems of implementation as these present themselves. Our justification for proposing what will be, in the long term, a minor financial adjustment, can be found in the letter and the spirit of the Special Projects Act: development efforts have failed precisely because planners have been unwilling to invest in the long-term social effectiveness of projects.

We recommend that the new boats be phased in, and the old boats phased out, over a three-year period - comfortably within the four-year deadline for installing the project. This will give the local people a better chance to come to terms with the social and political challenges pinpointed by the ISS report. Three years will allow time to strengthen the cooperative organization on which the project will depend, to construct supplementary enterprises, to mitigate the disruptive effects of hostility between Alpha and Beta, and to allow household members (men, women, and children) to adjust to their new roles. There is a real risk that immediate introduction of the new technology will place the richer and better informed members of the community at an unfair advantage. A step-by-step program of implementation will allow project management time to ensure that less advantaged members of the community have *privileged* access. Training can also be organized more rationally: stepping up the number of project participants over a three-year period will allow some members of the community to transfer skills to others rather than having everyone fumbling to learn from a small number of outsiders on the first day of the project.

Proponents of the basic IFI plan will complain about the economic cost of slowing down the project: delaying the introduction of each new boat reduces the total catch and the amount of processed fish sold, and thus the internal rate of return of the project as a whole. This problem is exacerbated by the fact that the factory is a "lumpy" investment: unlike the new fleet of boats, it cannot be introduced bit by bit to save costs. We would reply that we are essentially concerned to *remedy defects in the basic plan*: to assume that the IFI plan is optimal and that tinkering with the balance of economic costs and benefits will be to the detriment of the project is the sort of nonsense that the Special Projects Committee was established to correct.

*SPAC - **GROUP B***

We propose that operating the factory at reduced capacity for a couple of years is a small price to pay for getting the whole project off to a sound start. Since we are obliged to work within the basic economic agenda laid down by IFI, we propose that the capital and interest payments on the fish factory should be deferred for two years, (a) to buy time to organize the transition from the old to the new technology and (b) to release extra funds for local investment in the critical second year of the project. To pay for this, capital payments on the factory will be raised from 11% annually over 25 years, to 12% over 23 years. The reduction of a little under 12% of annual net profits is the price of installing the project in a more realistic and more socially and economically viable manner (see Table 5). In the long run the gradual, progressive approach which we are advocating will be less costly to the community and to Arcadia.

PROJECT SCHEDULE

Reorganization of fishing
Our program for the changeover to the new boats is indicated in Tables 1 and 4. Our intention has been to introduce enough new boats in the first year to get the project off to a safe but viable start and to keep as many of the old boats in operation for as long as possible. Only 26 boats will have to be sacrificed in the first year to provide crews for 12 new boats. This assumes that most of the 24 *qualified* seamen required for the new boats must be brought in from outside the area. By the fourth year most of these will have been replaced by local men.

In the second year the number of new boats will be increased to 28. Every year, each village will phase out the same number of boats as the other, and equal numbers of fishermen will be recruited to the new boats. Advised by the ISS report, we assume that opportunities for wage earning will provide the main stimulus for recruitment to the new crews and thereby the elimination of the old boats. Since it is unlikely that the Fishermen's Cooperative will have sufficient authority in the initial stages, the NFCU management will request the two

*SPAC - **GROUP B***

village councils to mediate in the selection process: for every three new crewmen proposed, they will be required to dispose of one old boat, arbitrating disputes as best they can. Management should strive to mix members of the two villages in each new crew to establish a fully integrated fleet. Since the goal of the project must be to move as rapidly as possible to the target of 10,000 tons of fish a year, additional new boats, beyond the suggested quota, could be added to the fleet during the course of the second year if enthusiasm was running high. We note that the delivery schedule for the Pisces craft is six months, allowing some flexibility in planning.

An important principle in this transitional process will be that the operators of the old boats must be persuaded to sell fresh fish directly to the factory rather than for sun curing. This is necessary to keep the operation of the new factory up to the highest possible levels. The price paid (A.0.20 per kilo) may be sufficient inducement, and as increasing numbers of women seek factory jobs, labor available for traditional processing will be cut. Although we anticipate a "domino" effect as more people join the new system and compete against the old, project management may have to devise some supplementary controls and/or incentives. Our schedule not only allows project management *time* to make these adjustments, deferring amortization releases extra *funds* for supplementary investment in the critical second year of project implementation.

We recognize that the persistence of old boats during the period of transition poses problems of control. Clearly, they will be put under increasing pressure from more efficient craft, which can easily displace them from the inshore fishing grounds. If (and only if) it proves necessary to provide inducements to abandon old boats and methods, we suggest a lottery, a prize of, say, A.20,000 being offered for all those relinquishing their boats to the NFC. Lacking information, we can only speculate about how these old boats could be disposed of safely, if not profitably. Possibly they could be sold by the NFC to other coastal communities still fishing in the traditional way. Stripped of net-stanchions and fishing gear, they might be kept for use on the river and along the shoreline or for entertaining tourists. A few of the finer specimens should be preserved for exhibition, perhaps as the nucleus of a local museum.

*SPAC - **GROUP B***

In proposing a gradual approach we have sought to mitigate the problem of policing the use of surviving old boats. The biggest reduction occurs in the third year, by which time attractive, alternative employment should be available. We suggest that at the end of the third year any remaining traditional boats should be completely barred from catching goleta. It would be the responsibility of the captain of each new vessel to identify and report transgressors to the project management, which would then apply penalties, such as suspension from the cooperative and thus exclusion from project benefits.

Reorganization of fish processing

The factory is the most costly and most intractable part of the project. Too little attention has been paid to the installation of the factory in the basic IFI plan. We are obliged to take a great deal for granted: we are, for example, surprised that the long-term gross cost should amount to as much as nine times that for the entire fishing fleet. Our proposal takes explicit and realistic account of the fact that, in terms of capital investment, the factory is the most important part of the project.

We recognize that our gradual approach applies more easily to installation of the new fleet than the factory. Although it is impractical to phase in the buildings, machinery, &c., the workforce should be adjusted to meet the increasing volume of fish over the three-year period (see Table 2). We have represented this as a simple progression, reckoning full-time wage rates. However, it will be desirable to involve as many women as possible in the factory from the earliest stage, to distract them from curing and selling fish in the old manner and to build up a reliable and experienced workforce. During the first three years, factory shifts should therefore be shortened to increase the number of employees. This will have the added advantage of allowing the women more time to adjust their domestic routines and establish new arrangements for child care, provisioning, &c.

Paying the full amortized price of the factory, according to the IFI plan, is a steady charge to the project of A.1,210,000 a year. As Tables 3(a) and 5(a) indicate, this is incompatible with our proposal to

*SPAC - **GROUP B***

phase the project in over three years. With only 12 new boats and a greatly reduced catch, the project as a whole would face a deficit of more than a million arenas in the first year. We therefore propose that capital and interest payments on the factory (not the boats) be deferred for the first two years and redistributed over the 23 remaining years of amortization. As Tables 3(b) and 5(b) indicate, the effect of this will be to raise the annual capital charge for the factory to 0.1196 per annum for the 23-year term, about 1% (A.110,000) more that the rate proposed by IFI, and to reduce the estimated profits for the project by 11.8% per annum.

The benefits of this financial adjustment in the critical initial phases of the project are very striking. Although factory profits in the first year are kept low by the heavy fixed costs, release from the burden of amortization in the second year *doubles* profits compared with the third and subsequent years. This provides, *at the right time*, additional funds for supplementary investment in the project - effectively an advance on future profits to secure investment in the critical phase of establishment. We will suggest how these resources should be invested in a later section of this proposal. However, it will be evident that effective management and public participation will depend on the development, during our phase-in period, of a robust cooperative organization.

COOPERATIVE ORGANIZATION

We believe it will not be difficult to make a virtue of the necessity to cooperate. We know of no better means of involving local people in development projects and of striking the right balance between equitable access to resources and efficient use of them. According to the ISS report, the people themselves agree that "more people should share in ownership of bigger boats."

Everyone born in the Alpha and Beta communities and over the age of 15, and everyone who has lived there for more than 15 years, will automatically become a member of a newly constituted branch of the National Fishermen's Cooperative. All others will be elected on a minimum vote of two-thirds of the membership.

*SPAC - **GROUP B***

There will, however, be two subdivisions of the cooperative: one exclusively for persons working in the fish processing factory, the other exclusively for people fishing. Each subdivision will elect a management committee for the new fleet and for the factory, on terms to be arranged with the NFCU. The two bodies will together constitute a plenary committee for management of the project as a whole.

Membership of each of these divisions will constitute a capital share, maturing in 25 years in the case of the factory and 10 years for the boats. Until they mature, shares will be transferable only through the agency of each subdivision of the NFC, which will have the right to reclaim shares of those who leave the project for any reason, paying appropriate compensation, and to reallocate such shares to others. Those who retire or become incapacitated may retain their share (and membership rights) or sell it back to the NFC. This form of shareholding will reinforce commitment to the project, stabilize NFC control, and act as a form of pensioning provision to members. It will also give younger people a firm stake in the future, strengthening loyalty and a sense of involvement. The ISS report notes that they, specifically, "seemed to relish the prospect of working... on a share-purchasing system."

Although these arrangements do not rule out the possibility of men working in the factory or women working on the boats, in effect the two subdivisions will be preponderantly female and male. Our purpose is twofold: to give strong, distinct economic and political powers to women, rooted in their previous control of fish marketing and processing, while leaving the door open for a reduction in the sexual segregation of work. We do not, in principle, approve of the plan to put men in supervisory positions in the factory, although there may be no way of avoiding this in the early stages of the project. If they are not community members they will receive wages but not shares. Trained members of the Cooperative should fill these positions as soon as possible. When the Cooperative divisions are functioning, they will have the right to adjust wage rates and terms of employment, within the budgetary constraints of the project.

Profits accruing to the boats and the factory will be in the hands of

SPAC - **GROUP B**

each subdivision of the Cooperative. This will place considerable resources, intended primarily for community welfare, at the disposal of the factory cooperative, and essentially in the hands of women. They will thus be empowered not only to direct funds to new essential services like care for children and the elderly but to provide loans for investment in new enterprises which may compensate for loss of income and opportunities in fish curing. For their part, men will be able to direct profits from fishing (see Table 4) to maintaining and improving the fleet and its equipment. Management should ensure that conspicuous use should be made of these funds to support the operation of the new vessels. We have in mind start-up costs for net purchase and maintenance, safety equipment, marine markers, &c., all of which should help to make the new system more attractive and more effective. In the basic IFI plan, provision for this seems inadequate.

Equity has been our watchword in drawing up this proposal. The ISS investigators uncovered fears among the poorer people that the rich would take over the new facilities; they felt that "more people should share in ownership of bigger boats." No doubt they will be happy to see this principle extended to the factory.

Every effort will be made to dissociate the new structure from past attempts at cooperation in the villages. The new Cooperative will provide a democratic political nexus for the new enlarged community of Alpha-Beta, with the capacity to incorporate but also to restrain established vested interests. Each subdivision will transect the two communities, helping to dissolve the distracting and counterproductive differences between them. There are indications that the women of these villages are practiced cooperators, sharing curing facilities and no doubt collaborating in fish marketing. We are therefore confident that a new alliance of women will forge bonds and encourage the construction of shared facilities which the community as a whole so urgently needs. We envisage a natural reduction in the activities and influence of the existing village committees.

We are aware of the checkered history of the cooperative movement in Arcadia but see many advantages in building on the "obligation to cooperate" which the ISS report assures us is a basic condition of the

*SPAC - **GROUP B***

project. Past failures have occurred mainly because there has been too little to cooperate *about:* too little investment, few plans, weak management, &c. This project offers many opportunities to make cooperativism work. The profits accruing to the two subdivisions of the NFC will inevitably undermine the power base of established groups, putting the greatest good democratically in the hands of the greatest number. A key element will be management: the project budget makes very generous provision for this, and every effort should be made to attract officials of the highest caliber.

SUBSIDIARY INVESTMENTS / DEVELOPMENT

Our aim is to keep both fish catch and employment up to the highest levels in the initial stages of the project. Under our scheme, the problem of unemployment is mitigated and its worst effect deferred to the third year. Accordingly, strategic use should be made of the exceptional A.1.4 million profit margin in the second year to develop subsidiary forms of employment. For example, the NFC should provide grants to establish enterprises of immediate value to the project, like retail shops, child and elder care services, mechanical repair facilities, &c. The Cooperative should establish firm collective patronage over contracts for maintenance, supplies, &c., favoring its own members with loans and assistance. In this way the project can discharge its responsibility to those members of the community not directly involved in fishing or fish processing.

It would be a contradiction in terms to imagine that any development effort can be instantaneous in its effects. Every healthy project is a process, hopefully extending far beyond the target dates of our plans. This is why we have been so concerned about scheduling transition in the first few years. It is vital to be able to respond flexibly to new and unanticipated needs and capacities within the community as technical transformations take effect. There is a particular need to plan for the next generation: the local NFC must establish youth programs, vocational schemes, &c. to support the future of the fishing industry and develop ancillary occupations. In this regard, full use should be made of the provision which the Special Projects Act makes for collaboration with the Education and Community Development

SPAC - **GROUP B**

Ministries. Here again, strong cooperative organization of the people themselves will be the key to fruitful collaboration with government agencies.

CONCLUSION

Viewing time as a scarce resource, we believe we have made sensible use of the four-year horizon for putting the project into effect. This is very much in keeping with government aspirations for new tactics in development initiatives. The Special Projects Act is seriously concerned to establish development projects which *work*, in contrast to so much of the impetuous efforts and undignified failures of the past. One thing we Arcadians have learned is that sound development cannot be rushed. It is surely worthwhile to devote just a small proportion of the budget of our projects to making sure that they are sustainable in the long term. This certainly requires additional thought and care. We make no apologies for the fact that our rescheduling proposals *complicate* the planning exercise: we would protest that the basic IFI scheme was too crudely simple in the first place. It would be grossly irresponsible to dump the new infrastructure and technology in Alpha and Beta and expect the people and the NFC to make it all work immediately. It is a cardinal responsibility of this Committee to insist on a closer and more durable commitment of planners.

It is possible that government might object that delayed implementation of the project cannot be justified because of the social costs as economists understand them, especially those associated with providing the basic infrastructure: the public might complain that the money could be put to better use somewhere else, rather than waiting for a handful of fishermen to take advantage of a great opportunity. We can only argue that it is in the spirit of the Special Projects Act to monitor closely expenditures on development and to take serious account of the interests of the local people. These "social costs," on which effective participation in the project will certainly depend, are inevitably highest in the initial phases. The profitability of the project in terms of net present value may be reduced in our three year phase-in, but reckoned over the long term -

*SPAC - **GROUP B***

the normal 30-year span of project planning - any economic loss will be heavily outweighed by the gains in establishing a viable investment.

We feel confident that our program is exemplary in all respects. In principle it is certainly transferable to other sites along the coast: a sound balance is struck between official control and opportunities for local adaptation. All projects, whether "Special" or not, depend fundamentally on the enthusiasm of the public response. It takes time for a reasoned commitment to the project to be established and for mutual trust to be consolidated. Instant, irrational enthusiasm is no basis for durable development. We believe that the Special Projects Initiative offers rare opportunities to buy a little time to ensure success by shifting material costs just a little in favor of social benefits.

*SPAC - **GROUP B***

Table 1 - BASIC SCHEDULE FOR FISHING

	Now	Year 1	Year 2	Year 3>
OLD BOATS:				
Number	140	114	72	0
Men employed	420	342	216	0
Catch (tons)	2,100	1,710	1,080	0
NEW BOATS:				
Number	-	12	28	40
Men employed	-	96	224	320
Catch (tons)	-	3,000	7,000	10,000
TOTALS:				
Men employed	420	438	440	320
Catch (tons)	2,100	4,710	8,080	10,000

Table 2 - BASIC SCHEDULE FOR FISH FACTORY

	Year 1	Year 2	Year 3>
Skilled workers	6	8	8
Wages (arenas)	37,500	50,000	50,000
Unskilled workers	50	80	100
Wages (arenas)	100,000	160,000	200,000
Total wages (arenas)	137,500	210,000	250,000
TOTAL fish sales (arenas) @ A.900 per ton	2,755,350	4,726,800	5,850,000

SPAC - **GROUP B**

Table 3 - RESCHEDULED ANNUAL ACCOUNT FOR FACTORY

(a) *Capital charge 0.11 over 25 years*

	Year 1	Year 2	Year 3>
Amortization	1,210,000	1,210,000	1,210,000
Other fixed costs*	1,600,000	1,600,000	1,600,000
Fish @ A.200/ton**	942,000	1,616,000	2,000,000
Wages	137,500	210,000	250,000
Total costs	3,889,500	4,636,000	5,060,000
Sales to AFC			
fillets @ A.900/ton	2,755,350	4,726,800	5,850,000
Profit (to NFC)	-1,134,150	90,800	790,000

(b) *Capital charge 0.12 over 23 years*

	Year 1	Year 2	Year 3>
Amortization	0	0	1,320,000
Other fixed costs*	1,600,000	1,600,000	1,600,000
Fish @ A.200/ton**	942,000	1,616,000	2,000,000
Wages	137,500	210,000	250,000
Total costs	2,679,500	3,426,000	5,170,000
Sales to AFC			
fillets @ A.900/ton	2,755,350	4,726,800	5,850,000
Profit (to NFC)	76,350	1,300,000	680,000

*   Other fixed costs include project administration, maintenance, fuel, and packaging.
** Comprises catch from both new and old boats.

SPAC - **GROUP B**

Table 4 - RESCHEDULED ANNUAL ACCOUNT FOR NEW BOATS

	Now	Year 1	Year 2	Year 3>
Amortization	0	97,800	228,200	326,000
Fuel, &c.	0	135,000	315,000	450,000
Wages @ A.27,000 per boat	0	324,000	756,000	1,080,000
Total costs	0	556,800	1,299,200	1,856,000
Sales @ A.200/ton to factory	0	600,000	1,400,000	2,000,000
Profit (to NFC)	0	43,200	100,800	144,000

Table 5 - SUMMARY: PROJECT PROFITS ACCRUING TO NFC

(a) Net profit WITHOUT deferred amortization

	Year 1	Year 2	Year 3>
Boats	43,200	100,800	144,000
Factory	-1,134,150	90,800	790,000
Project total	-1,090,950	191,600	934,000

(b) Net profit WITH deferred amortization

	Year 1	Year 2	Year 3>
Boats	43,200	100,800	144,000
Factory	76,350	1,300,000	680,000
Project total	119,550	1,400,000	824,000

*SPAC - **GROUP B***

SPECIAL PROJECTS ADVISORY COMMITTEE: THE ALPHA-BETA FISHERIES PROJECT

EVALUATION AND IMPLEMENTATION PROPOSAL BY GROUP C

INTRODUCTION

After much vigorous discussion, our group resolved that the proposed project for Alpha and Beta could make a positive contribution to relieving the notorious poverty of this region. Doubts were expressed that the technical specifications of the project, notably the choice of vessels and the scale and organization of the factory, allowed too little room for maneuver in the implementation process, from the point of view both of efficient management and of equitable local adaptation. Despite these and other problems with the plan, there was broad agreement that *some* far-reaching development scheme for this region is long overdue. Our group felt that the implementation process offered opportunities to redress the deficiencies of the basic plan, and to strengthen the *longer-term* prospects for success.

PROJECT CRITIQUE

We asked ourselves: Just how badly off are the people of Alpha and Beta today, and exactly how will their circumstances be improved by the project?

Current income per capita in the region is estimated to be among the lowest in Arcadia, about one-third of the national average. The data supplied indicate that the 206 households directly dependent on fishing generate a gross income of A.630,000 from sales of cured fish, i.e., about A.3,058 per household, or a mere A.437 per capita. In the proposed project, the wages paid for both fishing and processing amount to A.1,330,000. With approximately half (428) of the adult population employed in the new scheme, this suggests an annual income of A.10,902 for those households with both men and women employed in the project, or some A.1,557 per capita. This looks like a considerable improvement: a more than threefold increase in earnings, as predicted in the IFI report, which should take these people a little above the national average.

*SPAC - **GROUP C***

However, this is the most optimistic interpretation of available data on poverty and development prospects. These reckonings tell us too little about how people, wealth, and incomes are distributed now in the two villages and how they will be distributed in the future. Taking the entire population and total earnings from fishing, annual average income per capita would be A.367 now and A.775 in the future. In this more pessimistic account local incomes are barely doubled, leaving the population well below the national average and raising questions about the adequacy of project benefits.

However, a balanced evaluation must evoke social benefits beyond the compass of personal incomes. As part of the Special Projects package, these communities are promised government-subsidized improvements in health, education, and other services, from which everyone in the community is supposed to benefit, whether or not they are involved in fishing. If the proposed project is to apportion direct and indirect benefits to every member of these communities equally, strenuous efforts must be made from the outset to ensure that everyone has the same opportunity to participate. The basic plan, as it stands, offers no such safeguards, and if the distribution of gains is not carefully controlled, the dreary precedents of Third World development will assert themselves: the rich will get richer, the poor will get poorer, and the project will collapse.

Nor can we take for granted that the proposed distribution of costs and benefits between the community and outside agents is equitable. Members of our group have called into question (1) the Arcadian Fish Corporation's low factory gate fish prices; (2) the high administration and maintenance fees paid to the National Fishermen's Cooperative Union; and (3) what may be exorbitant interest rates for the processing plant. In these and other matters the local people are entirely at the mercy of government monopsonies and administrative control. We are very uneasy about appearing to work unquestioningly within the rubric of these figures, since no adequate justifications for these budgets are offered. Might the people not fare better by hiring their own managers, selling fish to commercial companies, and seeking mortgages in the private sector? If the Special Projects package denies such access, does this not go against official policies to promote democracy and free enterprise?

The Special Projects Act seeks to ensure that the most productive partnership between government and people is established

*SPAC - **GROUP C***

in every development project from the start. We doubt whether, in this case, local interests and initiatives have been adequately integrated into the planning process and thus whether we can expect the people of Alpha and Beta to respond to the proposals with enthusiasm. Fundamental decisions have already been made, and it is evidently the people who are expected to adjust to the plan, rather than vice versa. The choice of "Pisces" vessels and specification of the crewing arrangements have been made for the people rather than by them, and appear to have involved negotiations with a foreign government (Illyria) but not with the natives of Alpha and Beta. Importing technology has many implications for the project, for example, ruling out the possibility of developing a local boat building enterprise and making the local industry dependent on external and foreign sources for spare parts, servicing, &c.

In particular, we question the wisdom of putting the existing fleet out of commission and obliterating a product which is so well established in regional markets. We can assume that sun-cured fish is a valuable source of protein for rural Arcadians who will never be able to buy frozen fillets. Is cutting the supply of this commodity in accordance with the government's commitment to stimulate enterprise and promote welfare at the "grass roots"? Surely it is not the intention of the *Regional* Projects Division of the National Planning Commission to put regional markets out of business!

Confronted by all these doubts and constraints, we propose an implementation plan which seeks

(1) to ensure the equitable distribution of project benefits among all community members;

(2) to maximize control of these benefits by the local people themselves;

(3) to integrate the existing technical capacities of the local people into the project;

(4) to extend the opportunities for local initiatives in adapting and modifying the plan as it is being put into effect;

(5) to regard the project not as an instant transformation with an immediate schedule of costs and benefits but as a long-term process which must serve these villagers and Arcadia as a whole over several decades.

*SPAC - **GROUP C***

LINKING THE "TRADITIONAL" AND THE "MODERN"

Our group agreed readily on one fundamental matter: the distinction between "traditional" and "modern" in projects of this kind can be dangerously misleading. Development efforts have suffered too long from unthinking attitudes of "out with the old, in with the new." The notion that the motorized vessels should immediately replace the old boats has an extremely short sighted logic. Local people undoubtedly know more than the outside "experts" about the virtues of the existing boats and techniques of curing and marketing fish and may have excellent reasons for refusing to abandon the established system. They have been "farming" these waters with great skill for a long time. Can Arcadia afford to squander such valuable assets?

The price of sun-cured fish may be A.30 per 100 kilos less than the factory gate price for frozen fillets, but the value added remains essentially within the households which catch, dry, and distribute the product. Apart from the shock of abandoning such a valuable capital asset as the family boat, fishermen will with good reason wish to hedge their bets against commitment to a new and as yet unproven system. A plan which takes a much more continuous view of old and new technologies, and of the process of transition, will prove less disruptive in the short term, and more productive in the medium term, than a rapid and traumatic switch.

We therefore propose to retain one-third of the existing fleet at the start of the project. This will sustain a valuable element of diversity within the local economy which will actually enhance the prospects of the new system. The challenge of such a proposal is to ensure that it will not undermine the viability of the new system by over-fishing or by reducing the volume of fish delivered to the factory below the level for which its operation was designed. Since the new boats are scheduled to take the maximum catch, their number must be reduced if any old boats are to be retained. Likewise, continuing to produce sun-dried fish must entail some reduction in the supply of fresh fish to the factory.

The challenge is to calculate a balance which allows an optimal combination of the old and new systems. In doing this we have been concerned

(1) to retain the largest number of old boats *and* new boats
(2) to sustain full employment (420 fishermen)
(3) to sustain the maximum catch of 10,000 tons annually

*SPAC - **GROUP C***

(4) to direct the largest possible volume of fresh fish to the factory, keeping employment and productivity levels there as high as possible.

While new boats *must* dispose of their catch to the factory (a rule which should be easy enough to enforce), old boats *may* do so. On our reckoning (see appendix) 37 new boats may be combined with 50 old boats, producing respectively a catch of 9,250 tons and 750 tons, and employing respectively 296 and 150 fishermen. This actually exceeds the projected full employment total of 420 by 26 jobs, making allowance for the recruitment of outsiders to qualified navigational positions in the early stages of the project and the need to expand employment for the rising generation over the next few years. Sun-curing will continue to provide work for women, boosting employment levels above the 100 jobs provided in the factory. This will enhance women's options, allowing those with heavy domestic responsibilities to continue working on their own schedules within the household if they wish.

Tables 1 and 2 revise the operations accounts for the "Pisces" launches and the factory. They show a reduction in profits accruing to the NFC, when compared with the accounts proposed in the basic plan. This, we argue, is a modest price to pay for the longer-term benefits of providing a link between "traditional" and "modern" systems. While no more than 50 old boats must be allowed to fish, this number can be reduced if and when the attractions of working on the new vessels gain ground. The factory will operate with a minimum of 9,250 tons of fresh fish, which is not a drastic reduction. We assume that some proportion of the 15 tons caught annually by each "traditional" boat will be sold to the factory at the fixed rate of A.20 per 100 kilos.

However, our proposal has very significant implications for the employment of women. We are in effect trading off eight jobs in the factory (representing the 750 tons of fish "lost" for filleting) for continued employment for an estimated 135 women in the "traditional" sector: referring to the ISS report, we assume that 376 of the adult women come from "fishing households" and that a little more than one third of these will still be drying and marketing the fish from the 50 old boats. Thus, when the project starts we can ensure gainful employment for 235 women, more than doubling the rates under the basic plan. Considering that a large proportion of the 443

*SPAC - **GROUP C***

adult women in the two villages will not wish to seek factory work, for reasons of age, health, or other commitments, we feel confident that we will not be confronted with serious problems in selecting recruits for the factory. As a guide, we would suggest that women are employed strictly in order of ascending age (from 16 years), which should avoid arguments about which applicant from which household or village should be favored. It will also ensure an active and able-bodied work force.

Like all other aspects of the project, the success of these provisions will depend on strong management by the Cooperative. Initially a quota of 25 old boats from each village will be selected (by lottery, if necessary) and licensed by the Cooperative. They will be marked (like the new boats) with a conspicuous number. They will be restricted to fishing in an inshore area marked by buoys. Since the Cooperative will be obliged in any case to organize sectors at sea for the 37 new boats, the procedure is unlikely to seem discriminatory. If it appears at any stage that the "traditional" fleet is exceeding its quota of 750 tons, the markers will be moved to reduce their fishing grounds. We assume that the system will be to a large extent self-policing: each segment of the fleet will discourage the other from operating in its designated area. The Cooperative will have to develop means for arbitrating the disputes which will inevitably arise.

Our intention is not to prohibit the "evolution" of the old fleet into larger, mechanized vessels. It is healthy and appropriate to encourage local industry and innovation, even if it leads to the production of craft which rival or even displace the new boats. We envisage that the "fittest" old boats will survive and acquire licenses, and that at some stage it may be necessary to devise a system which allows the substitution, *pro rata*, of vessels of appropriate performance and capacity for the "Pisces" launches. Although a large proportion of the unlicensed boats will eventually rot, the rest (kept mainly for recreational and casual use) will serve as a reserve fleet. At any stage, the old boats will provide a buffer against mechanical and other failures with the new boats - a "safety-first" benefit not considered in the basic plan.

IMPLEMENTATION SCHEDULE
We propose that introduction of the new vessels and licensing of the old should be carried out as speedily as possible after the

SPAC - **GROUP C**

infrastructure is installed, to minimize losses on investment. We are confident that the balance we have struck (37 new boats, 50 old) anticipates the proportion of the work force which will wish to shift immediately to the new system. Our calculations are broadly in accordance with the preferences and attitudes elicited in the Institute of Social Studies survey.

COOPERATIVE OWNERSHIP AND MANAGEMENT
Strong Cooperative Society organization will be at the heart of any implementation plan for this project. In the interests of both efficiency and equity, we propose that a single reorganized branch of the National Fishermen's Cooperative Union will take control of the project and its benefits *in perpetuity*.

All persons in the communities ot Alpha and Beta over the age of 16 (the official minimum school leaving age) will be registered automatically as full voting members of the Cooperative. The Co-op will thus be rooted in the local population without regard to sex or age. Anyone not born in the community or who has not lived there for five consecutive years, may be elected to membership by majority vote. Anyone may opt out, or seek re-admission, at any time. It would be neither desirable nor practicable to restrict Co-op membership to those actively participating in the project, because the Co-op is charged with the obligation of helping to fund health and welfare services for the entire community from project earnings. Likewise, we cannot allow assets on which the community as a whole depends to devolve into private ownership.

Although we have heard much about the hazards of cooperative ownership and management, we are very optimistic about its application to this project. The spirit of cooperativism is more firmly established within the community than might appear at first sight. Fishermen everywhere are practiced cooperators: the peculiar hazards of their lives make this essential. The current membership of 21% in Beta and 33% in Alpha reported by the ISS are remarkably *high* rates, given that no externally organized development initiatives are currently in hand. Likewise, we consider it remarkable that as many as 28% of household heads currently favor cooperative ownership of the new vessels, given that no specific proposals have yet been put to them. Encouraging private ownership of the new boats could only be inequitable: it is quite unrealistic to suppose that an ordinary

SPAC - **GROUP C**

fisherman could afford one of the new boats, it would cost him 33 years' wages. Only those who are already wealthy, or who become wealthy by other means, could make such a bid. It is hardly surprising that the ISS survey should find that 67% of the heads of fishing households wanted private ownership of the new boats. These 138 men constitute just 8% of the population, the majority of whom would undoubtedly wish for less exclusive access to proprietary interests.

We are disturbed by the conspicuous lack of information about women's interests in cooperative participation: in what ways do women collaborate in the production and marketing of fish today, and how may this provide a basis for future cooperative organization? Likewise, the ISS survey is mute on questions of the ownership of the factory where, it is proposed, a quarter of the women will be employed. Of course, the arguments against private ownership apply *a fortiori* to this costly asset.

The long-term interdependence of factory and fleet lies at the heart of the project, and nothing can be gained from allowing any separation of controlling interests. In our proposal *all* men and women will share equally in the ownership of *all* capital assets. If men resent the fact that women will share responsibility for management of the new fleet, they must understand that this is nothing more than the price of admission to the modern world. In the new structure, one-person-one-vote may not end the war of the sexes, but it should at least put it on a more equal public footing. It appears that women now exert some considerable influence over economic processes in these communities, through their control of fish processing and marketing. It is essential that the Cooperative should take very explicit measures not only to protect the existing powers and privileges of women but also to *extend* those powers and privileges within the organization of the project. Development efforts in Arcadia and elsewhere have made it clear that this progressive change does not simply happen "naturally" but must be organized very consciously and explicitly.

We would point out that in our proposal people remain full members of the Cooperative until their death. This offers assurance for a segment of our population which is too often neglected: the elderly. We seek democratic safeguards for their welfare and dignity, through their share in the corporate enterprise.

*SPAC - **GROUP C***

The existing branches of the NFCU will be formally disbanded, and a new single branch established to operate the project and provide access to its benefits. It will act as corporate owner and manager of assets on behalf of the community and organize further investment and development within and beyond the 30-year lifespan of the project. While every effort should be made to emphasize the virtues of collective ownership and responsibility, individuals will be encouraged to benefit personally according to their direct involvement in the project. Once it has acquitted its responsibilities for paying capital, management, maintenance, and welfare charges, the Cooperative should have the freedom to disburse profits as its members think fit. We believe that the basic regulations of the cooperative movement in Arcadia and the good sense of the people will combine to ensure that selfish interests will not threaten the collective enterprise. A balance must be struck between adjusting wages and incentives for employees and distributing bonuses among general members. The present wage system is not set in tablets of stone: indeed, we can see no obvious reason for the 250% wage differential in the wages of "qualified" seamen and the "unskilled" fishermen (who presumably have lifetimes of knowledge and experience of local fishing conditions). The factory wage of A.40 per week seems inflexible and prejudiced against women. A system of piecework and bonuses would undoubtedly improve both efficiency and equity.

Although we lack the necessary detailed information, it is very probable that savings could be generated elsewhere in the project, for example, by reducing the large fixed allocations for administration and maintenance incorporated in the factory accounts. While seeking to involve as many local people as possible within the managerial and technical roles of the project, it would not be in the spirit of cooperativism to encourage significant differences of income and status within the project.

Every effort will be made to dissociate the Co-op from the existing community councils, whose membership is very narrowly restricted to the heads of boat-owning households. The activities and identity of the Co-op will focus on the new harbor and community center installations, emphasis being placed on the fact that these facilities are equidistant from the centers of Alpha and Beta. The new society will bear a "neutral" label selected by the members (e.g. "The

SPAC - **GROUP C**

Santa Maria Fishing Cooperative"), avoiding reference to either Alpha or Beta. A Cooperative council which represents all the adults of the new, amalgamated community will provide a much more efficient and democratic unit than the existing councils, and may eventually displace them within the local government structure.

INVESTMENT IN DIVERSIFICATION

A specific responsibility of the new Cooperative will be to develop additional economic ventures, with the intention of incorporating as many members of the community in project-related activities as possible. The Co-op might begin by exploring the marketing of sun-dried fish as a specialty product. Is there perhaps an epicure market, with export possibilities?

We particularly recommend that attention should be focused on the waste generated by the factory. While this could easily pose serious health and environmental hazards, it also constitutes a valuable resource from which the community could draw a profit, with some modest investment underwritten by the Cooperative. We have in mind the development of certain forms of shellfish and crustacean farming, and the processing of offal into agricultural fertilizer either for sale or for direct use in expanding horticulture in the two communities.

All that is required is some imagination and initiative. We hear, for example, that Koreans are very enthusiastic about pickled fish-guts. The Arcadian coast is already famous for its sauces based on fish byproducts. Here is another instance of how old expertise could be drawn into the new venture, helping to relieve the national trade deficit in an imaginative and ecologically sensible way.

The Cooperative could subsidize investment in all sorts of other local initiatives, ranging from retail stores to nursery care facilities for parents who become involved in fishing and factory work. It is clear that tourism also offers many prospects. The communities are endowed with the enviable resource of beaches which should become more accessible and perhaps cleaner when they are no longer so heavily deployed in the "traditional" fishing process. Some of the remaining small boats could be licensed to operate in the tourist domain. The Cooperative itself might invest in the construction of hotels. There is no doubt that as the transformation of Alpha and Beta proceeds, the picturesque busyness of the harbor and its

SPAC - **GROUP C**

environs will be an important attraction to visitors.

All these ventures are more than pipe dreams for the future expansion of wealth. They are fundamental responsibilities attached to the basic plan, to ensure that the Cooperative, and those directly engaged in the fishing industry, fulfill their obligations to the *entire* population of these villages and to the nation as a whole.

PROJECT REPLICATION

Our group was, to say the least, guarded about the prospects for "cloning" this project in other coastal areas of Arcadia. We are of the opinion that the "package" approach is not comfortably in accord with the Special Projects mission to involve local people in the planning and implementation of development.

We must surely seek economies of scale, but true progress does not come cheap. We would urge that the philosophy underlying our proposal is transferable to other contexts, but strengthening a project by grafting in local ideas, interests, and expertise inevitably demands deep, sympathetic knowledge of local circumstances. Indeed, we have complained that we lack sufficiently detailed information about these particular villages, *and* about the decisions embodied in the basic plan, to make adequate judgments about implementation. Our very ignorance is justification for our desire to restore at least some of the initiative for change and adaptation to the local people. And this, of course, is nothing more than what the Special Projects Act sets out to achieve.

CONCLUSION

The proposal of Group C is very much in tune with the Special Projects Act. Our aim is to enhance the efficiency, equity, and durability of the project by ensuring that it takes full account of the needs, capacities, and expressed interests of the local people.

We build on the existing economic system rather than seeking to overthrow it. The cost is a minor alteration in the basic plan: a reduction in the number of new vessels to accommodate one-third of the existing fishing fleet.

We secure very significant gains in employment, protecting the jobs of 120 fishermen and 135 women.

We seek to alleviate the trauma of change and to fortify the basic plan by weaving an established, indigenous pattern of

SPAC - **GROUP C**

development into a new program of economic and social change.

We sacrifice a few immediate gains to enhance development options later.

Our intention is to combine equitable involvement in the project with freedom to participate. Community members will remain joint proprietors of the very substantial assets and will manage them on democratic principles. Everyone will *benefit,* but individuals will draw *rewards* from the project according to what they contribute.

This interdependence of individual and communal interest will construct a durable social fabric which will sustain development for many years to come. We can think of no better foundation for the progress of our nation.

*SPAC - **GROUP C***

Table 1

Revised Annual Operations Account for Fish Processing Plant

Costs	Arenas
Amortization	1,210,000
Administration	300,000
Maintenance	500,000
Other (power, packaging, &c.)	800,000
Skilled labor	
8 @ A.125 per week	50,000
Unskilled labor	
92 @ A.40 per week	184,000
Inputs: 9,250 tons fish	
@ A.200 per ton from	
new and old vessels *	1,850,000
TOTAL	4,894,000

Sales	
6,012 tons of fish to AFC	
@ A.900 per ton	5,410,800
Profit (to NFC)	516,800

> *   Assumes that *none* of the traditional boats sells
> fish to the processing plant. Employment and
> profits can be raised in proportion to factory
> purchases from traditional boats.

SPAC - **GROUP C**

Table 2

Revised Annual Operations Account for 37 "Pisces" Vessels

	Per Boat (arenas)	Full Fleet (arenas)
Costs		
Amortization	8,150	301,550
Fuel, maintenance, &c.	11,250	416,250
Skilled labor	12,000	444,000
Unskilled labor	15,000	555,000
TOTAL	46,400	1,716,800
Sales		
9,250 tons @ A.200 per ton to processing plant	50,000	1,850,000
Profit (to NFC)	3,600	133,200

Appendix: <u>Calculating an optimal balance of old and new boats</u>

Goal: To find the largest number of both *old* and *new* boats which, combined, will provide the maximum catch (10,000 tons annually) and full employment (420 fishermen).

> t = "traditional" boats: crew = 3, catch = 15 tons a year.
> m = "modern" boats: crew = 8, catch = 250 tons a year.

Maximum Catch = 10,000 = 15t + 250m

$$2,000 = 3t + 50m$$

$$t = \frac{2,000 - 50m}{3}$$

Full Employment = 420 = 3t + 8m

$$420 = 3\frac{(200 - 50m)}{3} + 8m$$

$$420 = 2,000 - 50m + 8m$$

$$2,000 - 420 = 50m - 8m$$

$$1,580 = 42m$$

$$m = 37.6$$

We round this figure *down* to 37, to favor "traditional" boats:

$$t = \frac{2,000 - 50m}{3}$$

$$t = \frac{2,000 - 1850}{3}$$

$$t = 50$$

*SPAC - **GROUP C***

Summary:

Total Catch = 10,000
>   37 "modern" boats @ 250 tons each a year = 9,250 tons
>   50 "traditional" boats @ 15 tons each a year = 750 tons

Total Employment = 446
>   37 "modern" boats with crew of 8 = 296 men
>   50 "traditional" boats with crew of 3 = 150 men

Nb: based on reduced input of 9,250 tons, the number of *unskilled* operators in the fish processing plant is reduced by 8 to 92.

SPECIAL PROJECTS ADVISORY COMMITTEE: THE ALPHA-BETA FISHERIES PROJECT

EVALUATION AND IMPLEMENTATION PROPOSAL BY GROUP D

Our group is united in one conclusion: that the project should *not* proceed as planned.

It has not been easy to compose our report, partly because it is clear that a negative response is not expected of us, but also because we cannot and would not wish to pretend that we can speak with one voice. Indeed, one of our number offered a somewhat cynical yes vote: the plan should go ahead, if only to hasten the capitalist transformation of these communities. When they had been changed from an amorphous peasantry into a class-divided society, the ensuing conflict would speed the move to a more progressive, socialist society. Others among us doubt that such outcomes are predictable and believe that faith in communism is as unreliable as the more fashionable faith in free markets.

Everyone in our group was critical of the basic planning documents. These were seen to be founded on naive technocratic assumptions about economic and social development. We question the fundamental belief that the proposed changes are somehow a "natural" progression and that for their own good the people of Alpha and Beta need only to be nudged along a predetermined, universal path of progress. Although the Arcadian government is determined to come to grips with this sort of fallacy in development planning, we find the same old arrogant assumptions underlying the design of this small project: the agents of central government, advised by international "development specialists," know best how to improve the welfare of local people. Despite the Planning Commission's laborious efforts to meet the stipulations of the Special Projects Act, this plan shows very little comprehension of the lives of its victims, their identities and interests, their understandings of progress, and the

*SPAC - **GROUP D***

ways in which these contrast and conflict with the domineering world-view of privileged officials.

Emphasizing that we have an assortment of reasons for believing that the plan is misconceived and offering no pretense to unanimity, we have arranged our critique under three headings: (1) the technical base of the project; (2) its proposed transformation of the social relations of production and exchange; and (3) the ideological oppositions between planners and people which it embodies.

Finally, having arrested the project, we consider alternative prospects for change in this region: What should now be done?

(1) THE TECHNICAL BASE

Although the project is represented as building on existing technology, in fact it constitutes a radical breach. It seeks to replace existing material and human capital with imported technology over which the people will have little direct control, although they are being asked to foot the bill. The new vessels and factory will transform a relatively autonomous community into wage-labor force dependent on externally supplied and serviced capital. Even the "expertise" required to operate this capital will be imported, with little regard for existing competence.

The plan itself raises many technical doubts. Why are these people being obliged to buy foreign vessels rather than working with their own local materials and expertise? A two-hundred horsepower boat is no Titanic, and in their own domain these people are master boat builders. They are also master mariners: do the new boats really require a crew three times the size of the old? Or is this a ruse to give the impression of fuller employment? The capital charge for the fish factory is extraordinarily high, especially since its key operations are so labor-intensive. On the other hand, we have grave doubts that the budgetary provision for fishing gear is adequate: this will presumably have be drawn from the estimated annual profit of A.3,600 for each boat. If these are miscalculations or errors, it will of course be the people who will pay the costs and bear the blame for

SPAC - **GROUP D**

their "inefficiency" or "incompetence."

We are not offered a coherent account of the environmental impact of the project, doubtless because in national terms it is deemed "too small to matter." There is no indication that existing techniques are ecologically unsound, and it is outrageous to sweep them aside in favor of a new system which is supposedly "more efficient." The implications of piling up some 3,500 tons of fish offal each year are ignored. The plan makes profligate use of available resources. To proceed immediately to the maximum estimated catch of 10,000 tons is lethally improvident. This crude calculus threatens to despoil the patrimony of these communities, putting all available resources at the mercy of a single technical system which must displace all others.

The cavalier attitude of planners to the existing economic systems is much in evidence. The plan tacitly assumes that local consumption of fish, fresh and cured, will cease. This seems both improbable and impractical. The product is arbitrarily diverted to national and international markets, stripping the locality and the region of an important source of nourishment. Again, no account is offered of the disruption to traditional fishing while the infrastructure is being built. Carelessness about these costs, which local people must bear, contrasts with the fastidious accounting for the new vessels and factory.

(2) TRANSFORMATION OF ECONOMIC RELATIONS

The available documents make it very clear that the basic plan is not based on a clear understanding either of the structure of the existing economy, or of the nature of the transformations which are proposed.

We are concerned here with two different commodities, produced by different systems for different markets. Sun-dried fish is produced and marketed by households and consumed by mainly poorer Arcadians in the rural hinterland. The frozen fillets will be produced under factory conditions by wage-labor, for sale under state monopoly to privileged consumers in Arcadia and abroad.

*SPAC - **GROUP D***

Obsessed with the brave new world, the planners offer no account of the existing economy other than the tacit assumption that because the people are "poor" they are "underdeveloped." The panacea is the rapid introduction of capitalist relations of production.

The miscomprehension begins with a characteristic failure to recognize the peculiarities of fishing in relation to petty commodity production. It is readily assumed that fisherfolk are a variety of peasant, the global raw material for "development" efforts, and that the same political-economic tactics applied to producers of maize or cotton can be applied to producers of fish. Whether they work from tiny canoes or from deep-sea trawlers, fishermen do not appropriate nature in the way that farmers take possession of the land for cultivation. More akin to hunter-gatherer populations, they depend on skill, cooperation, and luck, and on the ownership of specialized forms of capital (boats, lines, nets) to extract a livelihood from nature. The plan makes brutal assumptions about the unimportance of existing factors and relations of production. Long-standing skills count for little, and to make way for the new vessels the existing technology will simply be eliminated. The burden of deciding how this act of expropriation will be performed (confiscation? forced sale? destruction?) is dumped on *us,* the Special Projects Advisory Committee, in the guise of a trivial administrative detail!

If the project is to make any pretense of building on the existing economy, it must make some effort to understand it. We are told that the relations of production and exchange are currently concentrated within family groups or households. Economic performance must therefore be understood in the context of these basic reproductive units, each "exploiting" its variable capacity according to its variable needs. Explaining relations within households over time is thus crucial to planning the development of fisheries. But the focus of the project is emphatically on external relations - with project management and state officials, between the two villages, within the Cooperative Society, etc.

We are told that there is a gendered division of labor in Alpha and Beta characteristic of fishing communities, with men collecting the raw material and women processing and distributing it. Typically, we

SPAC - **GROUP D**

hear most about the male activities, in reference to both the existing economy and the development plan. We are told virtually nothing about women's work, the curing and marketing of fish. This is tacitly dismissed as the old retrograde "traditional" system which will be steamrollered out of existence by the new economy - along with the established roles, skills, interests, and identities of women themselves.

The project is predicated on the familiar, outrageous assumption that women will be rescued from some sort of "unemployment" or "underemployment" and have bestowed on them the benefits of a wage. Their domestic roles, now and in the future, pass without comment. Knowing next to nothing about the old system, we can only guess how they will have to adapt to factory work. Having made no effort to compute women's earnings under the existing system, on what basis can the IFI declare in their report that "direct wage earnings of women will be increased"? Closer consideration of current circumstances might reveal that women, controlling the sales of dried fish and the flow of income into the community, in some fashion provide "wages" for men.

The plan perpetuates crude, stereotypical understandings of the subordinate status of women and naively assumes that they will be better off under the new system than the old. This is based on the bland assumption that the gains from a massively increased fish catch will trickle out to all, without regard to the existing and the emerging relations of production, reproduction, and exchange. The project proposes to improve the lot of women by shutting them up together in a shed all day, where they will cut up fish for less than one arena an hour. By sleight of hand, this expansion of female "employment" is represented as compensating for male redundancy as the new boats are phased in (see table 7 of the IFI Report). The reality is net job loss, and loss of income, for men and women. Selling their labor for cash in the factory, women will be alienated from the product, their families, and themselves. The only glimmer of hope is that, concentrated in such a grim working environment, they will quickly perceive the injustice of their circumstances, and take collective action to remedy it.

SPAC - **GROUP D**

Perhaps the greatest confidence trick is the insistence on cooperative management for the project. Masquerading as "collective ownership," the NFC is simply an instrument for the appropriation of labor by agents of the state, in exchange for vague promises about proprietary rights at some distant date (10 years, 25 years) when boats and factory are reaching the end of their useful lives. The plan specifies that the project will not be run by a democratic forum of the people but by highly paid outsiders. The state-sponsored ideology of cooperativism assumes that local branches build on the "natural" propensity for "cooperation" among simple rustic folk. This is a ridiculous, patronizing myth. Like cooperatives around the world, the NFC will in reality depend on private greed as the inducement to participate. In the new regime the prosperous will prosper, controlling power and wealth by commandeering offices and resources, as they did in the past. Starting a new club will not change human nature.

In sum, in the guise of "development," the people of Alpha and Beta are expected to switch "voluntarily" from a domestic petty commodity mode of production into fully fledged capitalism, under the patronage of the National Fishermen's Cooperative Union. Making a set of supposedly simple but profitable adjustments to their way of life, the people will have to make a historic leap which has proved disastrous for rural people in similar contexts around the world. Have the past three decades of "Green Revolution," "Modernization," and similar claptrap taught us nothing? Why should we inflict the same traumas on the people of Alpha and Beta?

(3) THE HEGEMONY OF PLANNED DEVELOPMENT

"Development" without some strong ideological basis is unthinkable and undoable. Our government, like any other that is pursuing progress, must sell its vision to the people in clear and confident terms. Fundamental ideas must be translated into policies, and policies into unequivocal plans of action. Watchwords and catch-phrases are vital in efforts to capture the imagination of the public and to draw their energies into development efforts. None of this we would deny. Ideology is a resource which every government must manipulate if it is to retain its authority.

SPAC - **GROUP D**

We are, however, deeply suspicious of rhetoric which is deceptive or void of practical meaning. Bombastic words which distort truth, or disguise unsavory intentions, have no place in our development efforts. We cannot afford to assume that the public is gullible. Some of them may enjoy the phallic thrust of the slogan "Forward and Upward," but everyone has learned that officials say one thing and do another. If we do not watch our words, people will quickly lose faith in our efforts to plan their progress.

The language of the Alpha-Beta documents is shot through with naive and deceptive rhetoric which calls to question the basic purposes of "development." The people are being offered brute capitalism in the liberal rhetoric of reform and soft-core socialism. The key document is the International Fisheries Institute report which, under the pretext of proposing options for development, actually circumscribes them rigidly in a few paragraphs. Arbitrary decisions are dressed up as technical expediencies: the type and number of new vessels, the organization of labor and its rates of remuneration, the size of the harbor, the location of the community center, and so on. Here is a classic example of technocratic hegemony - the voice of the economist haranguing all other parties in the development game. Absolute commitment to the values of "free market enterprise" is thinly disguised by appeals to the need to eliminate "poverty" - bluntly construed as low cash income. No alternative definitions and strategies are entertained. We might shrug off such mindless bullying as a humdrum feature of development planning everywhere, were it not for the fact that the Arcadian government has made such an issue of taking account of the interests of local people.

We can, frankly, see no serious evidence of such a concern. Instead of the voice of the people we are offered the pseudo-science of sociology, a clutch of bourgeois opinions dressed up in a report by the university's Institute of Social Studies. This false exercise in democracy pretends to measure "opinions" scientifically - "facts" are dressed up in figures. What meaning are we to attach to the "fact" that 68% of the total adult population of the two villages responded positively to the suggestion that "all things considered" they would be "better off when the new project is established" than they "are now"? Does this mean that the project will be 68% successful? By what

*SPAC - **GROUP D***

feat of the imagination can simple fishermen consider "all things" in making judgments of this kind? What weight can we attach to an opinion about a future which has not been explained to them in any detail, and which in the minds of planners themselves is thoroughly uncertain? These answers reduce the voice of the people to incoherent idiocy. Such "research" tactics do not allow the people to articulate their interests in any meaningful way; they solicit opinions in the most constrained manner and then have the effrontery to translate these opinions into a "vote." It is tacitly assumed that a simple majority is sufficiently eloquent, but what of the 45% of adults over 45 who appear to be negatively disposed to the project? Might this "minority" not exercise the authority of their years to trash the entire project? These computations have little to do with "democracy," and nothing at all to do with the complex of statuses and interests which define people and their actions in local communities. The reality of this exercise is a grave act of disenfranchisement, reducing real voices to gobbledygook.

As we have indicated, what is *omitted* from the documents is as eloquent as what is insistently declared. The ISS report works to a narrow functionalist agenda, seeing kinship, household headship, leadership, religion, etc. as keys to social structure, and regarding aspects of them as "obstacles" to the plan. Conflict is regarded as a pathology rather than inevitable to the process of change: it is construed as oppositions between the generations and between the two communities. Emerging differences of *class,* the polarization of rich and poor which is an inevitable part of any process of "development," are virtually ignored. Section (c) of the report, "The Distribution of Benefits," regurgitates pieces of hegemonic discourse (the awful slogan "All Arcadia for All Arcadians") but says nothing of observational or predictive value. Lapsing again into the numbers game, the section observes that local people fear that they will be invaded by outsiders.

The great irony is that this fear is cast for them by the ISS interrogators as wicked aliens stealing the jobs of local people. Pity those poor souls, trickling in from other parts of Arcadia in search of miserable wages in this notoriously depressed region! The ISS makes no allusion to those *other* outsiders whom the people of Alpha and

*SPAC - **GROUP D***

Beta should more justly dread: the ruling class of officials and politicians who plot their fate from the distant capital. These are the oligarchs who stuff their own bellies with cheap fish and fill the heads of the people who have produced it at massive human cost with utopian fantasies of wealth and happiness.

If "the people" are to participate fully and freely in the planning process, as this government hopes they might, the process itself will have to be demystified. But this may be too much to hope for. No hegemony is ever relinquished without a grand historical struggle.

(4) WHAT IS TO BE DONE?

Before we can pretend to help these two communities, we must be sure that we understand the problems to which our solution of "development" is being applied. In the IFI and ISS reports, the problem is perceived as "poverty," but in the very constricted terms of income deficiency. The remedy is income growth, through investment in local enterprise which expands opportunities for wage-earning and - a more distant prospect - capital acquisition. Both reports tacitly accept the creed of the benign, invisible hand of the market, shifting to the level of project implementation the problem of "ensuring equity" in the distribution of benefits. Too late! The terms of the project have already been dictated.

Beyond income, the realities of poverty and underdevelopment are barely touched upon in the project documents. We are told nothing specific about the health and nutritional status of the people of Alpha and Beta or of the welfare services available to them. What medical facilities are currently available? The introduction of a basic grade 4 clinic suggests that they have none. What provision, if any, is made for care of the dependent elderly and the young? And what specific allowance has been made for such provision in the plan?

There is no information about existing schools, levels of attendance and attainment, etc., and no proposals about how these should be improved in the context of the project. In references to the proposed community center, which will house facilities operated by the

*SPAC - **GROUP D***

Ministries of Health and of Community Development (with heavy subsidies from the project itself), there is only vague mention of "technical training." Educational facilities, for adults as well as children, are of prime importance if these people are to participate knowledgeably in decisions about their own future.

In sum, it is clear that virtually no effort has been made to solicit from the local people *their* ideas about their needs and the solutions which *they* envisage. As a small step towards remedying this, we would insist that the next meeting of the Special Projects Advisory Committee be conducted in the Alpha-Beta locality, preferably at the site of the proposed community center, which the project planners have touted as neutral territory. Further discussion will thus be conducted in full view and within earshot of the people whose lives are to be changed. Let us submit our arguments, pro and con, to this critical test!

Until more thorough inquiries have been made about these meanings of "development," and until local interests can be articulated more clearly, the government should concentrate on providing these impoverished communities, and others like them throughout Arcadia, with the basic social services which they should by rights have had long ago: adequate access by road and sea, provided by the Public Works Department; adequate medical and social welfare facilities; adequate schools; fair access to public utilities. It is outrageous to insist that the only way neglected villages like Alpha and Beta can acquire basic services enjoyed by the majority of Arcadians elsewhere is by selling themselves to a scheme which will strip them of the few assets they currently enjoy.

Tear up the plans for the new boats and factory - they portend only dependence, debt, and wage-servitude. Authentic "development" is already under way in Alpha and Beta - larger boats, outboard motors, vehicular transport of the dried fish, etc. Rebuild the road, the bridge, and a serviceable quay for larger boats. Build the clinic and community center - and a new school. These will enable the people of Alpha and Beta to take their fate into their own hands. But do not regard these as gifts from a charitable government. They are simply some small compensation for many years of criminal neglect.

SPAC - ***GROUP D***

Forward Upward Outward

PART THREE: THE EXERCISE

PETITION FROM THE ELDERS OF BETA TOWN
IN THE DISTRICT OF KAPPA
TO HIS SUPREME EXCELLENCY THE PRESIDENT OF THE
REPUBLIC OF ARCADIA, DOCTOR NAPOLEON MINES.

Your Respected Excellency,

WHEREAS from time immemorial our ancestors lived
without dependence or incumbrance upon others, drawing
fish from the sea which beats upon the shores of this,
our beautiful country,

AND WHEREAS through Your famous privileges and bene-
factions plans are now afoot to bring a Great Development to our people, which will enrich our children
and our grandchildren,

AND WHEREAS for many generations our people have
struggled against the tyranny of our neighbors in
Alpha Town, who wish to claim for themselves the sea
from which we draw our fish and the air we breathe,

WE MOST EARNESTLY BESEECH AND REQUEST YOUR EXCELLENCY
that You use Your inestimable Offices to bring to the
people of Beta Town a Development which is our own,
and which can benefit ourselves and our children, and
cannot be used as an instrument in the hands of the
elders of Alpha Town to abuse and dominate us as we
have been abused and dominated for generations.

IN TOKEN OF WHICH we will guarantee your Excellency
every commitment of loyalty and devotion, as we have
always done, and which we shall continue to do through
out what we pray will be a long and prosperous Reign
for your Excellency.

SIGNED this 30th day of March 1995, for and on
behalf of the ELDERS OF BETA TOWN, in the District
of Kappa, in the Republic of Arcadia:

CLERK, and Schoolteacher, Beta Town.

PRESIDENT SPEAKS OUT ON URGENCY OF LOCAL DEVELOPMENT

Metropole - Tuesday

At a reception today for the Japanese Trade Delegation, His Excellency the President, Napoleon C. Mines, spoke of Government commitment to "eliminating the grave embarrassment of poverty from the shores of Arcadia." The key, he explained, was to concentrate investment on neglected human resources.

His Excellency cited a project in the final stages of preparation to develop the fishing industry in two coastal communities of Kappa District. The local people had been mobilised, he informed the Japanese visitors, and the Government had committed a vital injection of funds and expertise for the project.

The President likened the Government's "Special Regional Projects Initiative" to a military SWAT team, working swiftly and efficiently to bring the right kind of project to the neediest people.

"We have to stop the arguments, cut the red tape, and deliver the goods," he declared.

Nevertheless, the President cautioned, development efforts can only succeed if they respond to the expressed needs of the people. Arcadians can be justly proud of their efficient advisory and consultative process. His Excellency drew attention to the panel of ordinary citizens convened a year ago to advise on the design and implementation of Special Projects for backward regions.

"My government has made strenuous efforts to open up the poorest and most isolated parts of the country to the benefits of economic development," the President told the Japanese visitors.

"The surest route to progress for Arcadia as a whole is to help ordinary people take advantage of the new climate of free commerce which is sweeping the world."

The Exercise

Playing the Game

In this book you are invited to play a game. As in all games, you must decide how seriously you want to play. One thing we know very well: Games can easily draw us into their own reality, raising our passions and our blood pressure. The ability to engage so readily in fantasy is a marvelous human gift that can be turned to great advantage in education and intellectual exploration. A sense of subjective involvement can enliven what might otherwise be dry, objective study. Games may be especially helpful when we are trying, like anthropologists, to understand the circumstances of people who lead very different lives, encouraging us to project our minds into the experiences of others. This is especially true if we are trying to bridge the conceptual gap between people who live in poor communities in distant parts of the world and those of us closer to the centers of power. Unless we take better account of these diverse points of view, we are unlikely to be able to propose effective remedies to the problems of poverty or to discover what sorts of "development" are preferable or practicable.

To enjoy playing this game, as any other, you have to understand the goals, rules, and relationships among the players. These are introduced in the first part of the book, "Specifications." These documents contrive a role for you: a member of the Arcadian public who has been appointed by the president's office to join the Special Projects Advisory Committee. You should spend a little time figuring out what this implies (in a real situation a layperson involved in this way might feel equally uncertain or perplexed). But you also have to get a feeling for tactics, for the arts of competition. The proposals in the second part of the book illustrate different strategies, and now you are invited to make a play of your own.

The way the game is set up may either please or annoy you, and you may like or dislike the stories I have told. If you know more about fish or boats or factories or economics than I do, you may be dogged by some technical illogicality that makes nonsense of the whole exercise for you. I submit that accounting for such a reaction is also part of the learning exercise. Even if you don't make much headway with the development dilemmas set out in the text, cataloguing the things that don't ring true can be an illuminating exercise in itself. Experience suggests, however, that credibility is less a problem than credulousness in games like this. The game acquires a "reality" of its own, despite the wholly fictitious nature of the exercise. As in "Dungeons and Dragons" or major league baseball, it is difficult to moderate the enthusiasm of certain players with the plea that "it's only a game!"

A basic purpose of this exercise is to bring the player to terms with these sublime attitudes and subjective dispositions. Ultimately, it is what *you* think and believe that matters. What anyone represented in the project documents (essentially me) "thought" or "believed" is only a catalyst. In completing your consideration of the Alpha-Beta project, you will therefore be prompted to account for your own views, implicit as well as explicit, about "development" and to try to explain why you hold *these* attitudes rather than others.

To set the ball rolling, here are a few questions that may help you come to terms with your intuitive feelings about welfare, progress, equity, efficiency, and some of the other values that weave in and out of the Alpha-Beta project documents.

- Which is the more important driving force in human progress: concern for others or personal greed?
- What is the main cause of poverty? Lack of economic resources? Inadequate technology? Abuse of power? Ignorance? Laziness? Traditional social values?
- To what extent does effective development depend on government control of the economy? Which alternative offers better guarantees of progress: unrestricted markets or tough government? How compatible are these in the pursuit of progress? Should government organize development directly or subsidize private interests to do the job?
- Does economic development inevitably make some people richer and other people poorer? If so, is this good or bad?
- Who knows best about development? Ordinary individual citizens? Qualified specialists? Elected politicians?
- Which is the best sponsor for development efforts? Big business? International aid agencies? The national government?

- Is it possible to plan development scientifically, in a politically neutral way? Who should make the key decisions in development—scientists or politicians?
- Which is likely to be more successful in the long term: development organized by central government or development organized by local government?
- Is a strong, authoritarian government likely to achieve more effective development than one that depends on voluntary participation? Which is more likely to succeed: one dictator or numerous popular committees?
- Which should be the higher priority: conservation of natural resources for use in the long term or exploitation of these resources to increase wealth and eliminate poverty today?
- Can you specify what you mean by the terms "poverty," "development," "underdevelopment," "progress," "social welfare"?

- What is the most important question missing from this list?
- Reviewing your responses to these questions, how would you label yourself politically and ideologically?
- Do you feel happy or uncomfortable about this identity? Or about being asked to identify yourself in this way?

Interpreting the Documents

It should be clear that the basic planning documents (especially the IFI and ISS reports) and the four proposals (A, B, C, and D) express different sorts of attitudes toward development in general and toward this project in particular. They are loaded with assumptions about what is right and wrong and what is or is not likely to succeed. Understanding the relationship between your own views and those expressed in the documents is an important step in drawing up your own recommendations about the project. Here are some questions that may help you to organize your thoughts:

- What sorts of attitudes prevail in the Arcadian Planning Commission, and what values underlie the IFI report? To what extent, for example, do they see free enterprise rather than government intervention as a remedy for poverty?
- Can you find an appropriate ideological label—for example, "liberal," "socialist," "conservative," "populist"—for the IFI report? And for

the ISS report? Be specific about which particular aspects of each report would merit such a tag.

- Would you use the same label for your own opinions about development?
- Do you think it's wrong to put labels on ideas like this? Why?

To piece together the different attitudes and opinions, you will find it helpful to review who the actors and agencies involved in the Alpha-Beta project are. Sketch out a hierarchy in the manner of a flow chart, suggesting who has authority over whom and who initiates activity for whom. Don't forget to include yourself in the diagram. Think very broadly about the different actors in this arena: the president of Arcadia and the elders of Alpha, the anonymous authors of the IFI report and Mr. Sifer of the Regional Planning Division, "Maria" in the travel article and the group that compiled proposal C.

Bear in mind the time factor in interpreting these relationships. Not all parties are in play simultaneously: The Regional Projects Division is involved more or less continuously throughout the specified life of the project, but the task of IFI is already accomplished, and the new branch of the NFC has yet to be established. Consider also the *extent* to which different groups are involved: Presumably the people of Alpha and Beta are most thoroughly and intensely engaged. The president seems concerned about the project, but his interest in it is not at all the same as someone in the Planning Commission or a citizen of Beta.

- How much does each party seem to know about the others (e.g., the IFI about the women of Alpha, or the president about SPAC)?
- How does this (lack of) knowledge affect how the project is being organized?
- Which party do you think *you* can most comfortably or knowledgeably identify with? Why?
- How do the limits of your own knowledge affect the advice you can deliver?

By filtering the "facts," those who assemble planning documents may seek (consciously or otherwise) to move decisions in a particular direction.

- In what ways do you think choices about the project are already preempted? Who did it—how, when, and why?

- How do the decisions about technology, management, and so forth in the IFI report affect your opportunities, as an SPAC member, to make proposals of your own?
- On what specific matters do you think you are being led or misled by the planning documents?
- How does your assessment of this affect how you compose your own proposal?

Evaluate the reasoning in the basic IFI plan:

- In your own judgment do the benefits justify the costs?
- What kinds of costs and benefits are explicitly factored into the reckoning of whether to proceed with the project?
- Do you believe there are *implicit* costs and benefits not accounted for with sufficient clarity?
- How much weight should be attached to numbers (wages, profits, boats, employees, etc.) and how much to qualities (security, leisure, happiness, etc.)?
- Within the limitations of time and cost, how could the IFI report have provided a better basis for judgments about the project?

Consider the relationship between the IFI report and the ISS report:

- Between the two documents, how well are economic and social concerns balanced? Note that one followed the other: The IFI report initiated the ISS report. Should economic criteria have priority over social criteria?
- How might a social plan set the terms for an economic report?
- Within the limitations of time and resources, how could the ISS report have provided a better basis for judgments about the project?
- How dependable is the information in the ISS report? Note that some effort was made to balance qualitative, descriptive information about the two communities and quantitative information relating especially to opinions. How much weight do you attach to each sort of information? Do you feel the need for more of one or the other?
- Would a more comprehensive breakdown of census material (age, sex, residence, etc.) have helped you? How?
- Do you believe the quality of life in Alpha and Beta and people's aspirations toward a better life are adequately represented in the ISS report?

- How do you think such matters could be better expressed in documents of this kind?

As in real life, the effectiveness of your role as a planner depends on how much you know and thus on how informative the documents are. As a member of an advisory committee dealing with a small project like this, you are probably being offered an unusually generous amount of information. For example, the ISS report is based on a full census of the two communities, not just a sample survey. You should certainly make note of frustrating data gaps, but remember it is probably too late to insist in your proposal on the collection of extra information. Who would pay for it? On what issues do you consider you have too much and too little basic information? Too much data complicates decisions, too little makes choices oversimplified and arbitrary.

Consider how you will come to terms with your own role as a member of the Special Projects Advisory Committee:

- You have apparently been chosen as an "ordinary Arcadian." What do you think this actually implies? What sort of behavior is expected of you?
- You had the honor of being appointed through the president's office. How do you imagine this came about? To what extent might this enhance or curtail your ability to work as a free agent? Are agents ever free in such circumstances?
- What sort of people do you think your colleagues will be?
- How will you get on with them when you are closeted together in a committee room? As a new member, might you find yourself playing an arbitrating or mediating role among the four groups? Will you take a side? Or will you try to sell some new proposal of your own?
- What sort of powers do you think SPAC has? Is its advice purely cosmetic, or does it have real clout? How constructive or destructive can you, and SPAC, be?
- What are the responsibilities of SPAC members? Will these end at the next meeting, when the basic decisions about the Alpha-Beta project are made? *Should* SPAC remain accountable while the project is being implemented?

You should try to be clear not simply about your own visceral inclinations but about what you think is expected of you in SPAC. How would you distinguish between what you really feel and what you ought to say?

In composing your proposal you should bear in mind the need to express your views persuasively but temperately. As a citizen of Arcadia, if you express certain strong opinions (*which*, do you think?) too frankly, you might end up in jail.

- To whom are you primarily responsible?
- With whom should your loyalties lie in the first instance? The Planning Commission? The president? If you answer simply "the people," *which* people? The people of Alpha or Beta? The women? The poor? All Arcadians?

Every level in this set of values matters if we are concerned to understand what development is about and how it should be done. Ultimately everything between the covers of this book is configured by a particular view of the world (mine). You may end up rejecting me, Arcadia, and the predicament of the people of Alpha and Beta lock, stock, and barrel. At least you will have had the opportunity, and perhaps the satisfaction, of explaining why.

Drafting Your Proposal

Take your cues, as a new recruit to SPAC, from the documents describing the state of play now—especially the *agenda* set for the upcoming (July 14) meeting of SPAC.

Remember the stage at which you have been drawn into this process and the role you are expected to play: You have been appointed to SPAC between the first and second (May 21 and July 14) meetings dealing with the Alpha-Beta project. You were not party to the discussion that led up to the proposals drawn up by subgroups A, B, C, and D, but you will be party to the discussions that ensue.

Remember, too, that the function of SPAC is advisory: It does not necessarily have the last word on whether or how the project will be implemented; it must seek to persuade the Planning Commission and ultimately the Arcadian government. Any proposal emanating from SPAC is unlikely to cut much ice if it is either too bombastic or too insipid. An account that offers few opinions or pays little attention to detail is unlikely to convince the Planning Commission that you are taking your SPAC responsibilities seriously. By the same token, a document that shreds the basic plan and blasts government policy is unlikely to go down very well in the president's office.

SPAC is only one link in the planning process. It is involved quite near the end of a lengthy series of considerations. This constrains the choices open to the committee: It can either accept or reject the basic plan and, if it accepts the plan, it must specify how the project should be put into effect. SPAC cannot, at this stage, reinvent the policy and the technical principles of the project. If you want the project to proceed, the best you can do is to suggest modifications—precisely and concisely—on the basis of *existing* information.

If you recommend rejection, you will have to explain *very persuasively* why. A vague queasiness is not sufficient grounds to dismiss a project on which a large amount of time, resources, and effort have already been expended. The heavy expenditure on planning, before the first brick is laid and the first dollar earned, constrains the choices about whether and how to proceed. We have been told quite forcibly that cutting down on waste is a central concern of the Special Projects Initiative. If you wish to propose modifications to the basic plan, bear in mind that the budget is not expandable and that additional costs must be set against specified savings.

Discussion at the forthcoming meeting of SPAC will center on the four proposals, A, B, C, and D, that compose the second part of this book. They should trigger your imagination and inspire to you make a proposal of your own.

- What distinguishes one proposal from the others?
- Which is more likely to achieve its own goals or the goals of the basic plan?
- Can you explain why you think one proposal or parts of a proposal are "right" and others "wrong"?
- How would you rate the various proposals in terms of simplicity and complexity? Do you incline to the view that simple solutions are best? Or would you say that effective plans for development must inevitably be complicated?
- Which proposal do you believe is most in accordance with your own views about development and how it should be done? Don't be satisfied with gut feelings, weak or strong. If something in one of the project documents makes you indignant, try to explain calmly what is wrong and why it is unjust or irrational or ineffective.
- Devise a title that identifies the intentions underlying each proposal. Can you apply ideological labels like "liberal," "socialist," "populist," or "conservative" to them? Be specific about which aspects of a proposal would merit such a tag.
- Can you detect inconsistencies within each proposal—for example, one recommendation that contradicts another?

- Take the standpoint of Group A and criticize the proposal of each of the other groups from this particular perspective. Then do the same from the standpoint of each of the other groups in turn. For example, what sorts of conversation can you imagine developing around the committee table between the people in Group B and the people in Group D?
- Can elements of the four proposals be reconciled within the form of a proposal of your own? How would you set about persuading the people in each of the four Groups?

Consider how the basic planning documents (especially the IFI and ISS reports) are criticized in the four proposals:

- Are some proposals too critical and others too uncritical? Explain your judgment.
- Which criticisms strike you as valid and which invalid—and why?
- Consider how *little* of the basic information (in the IFI and ISS reports) is actually used in each proposal. Note how different pieces of information are picked up in each proposal and how the same piece of information may be interpreted in quite different ways. Which "facts" that you consider important do the four groups ignore or manipulate?
- In composing your proposal, what sorts of information are *you* ignoring or manipulating? Can you explain why you are doing this?

After all this catechism, you should be impatient to put forward your own evaluation of the plan for Alpha and Beta and your proposal for implementation. Here, to prompt you in this task, is a series of questions under headings that suggest debate. The readings at the end of the book should help you clarify your thoughts on specific issues and encourage you to pursue matters of special interest. Even if you do not draft an evaluation and proposal for the Alpha-Beta project, either by yourself or in a discussion group, you may like to respond to each of these topics in the form of an essay.

Poverty and Progress

- In what ways do the basic plan and the various proposals for implementation solve the predicament of poverty?
- How, in this context, would you define "poverty"?
- How would you recognize that it had been eliminated?

Efficiency and Equity

- Are efficient development and equitable development compatible?
- Do the proposals for development in Alpha and Beta suggest that increased inequality is the price that must be paid for economic development?

Women and Men

- What are the advantages and disadvantages to women in the proposals for the project in Alpha and Beta?
- What recommendations would you make to guarantee that women will benefit from the project rather than becoming its victims?

Techniques and Politics

- To what extent will the success of the project depend on the right technology on the one hand or the right social values on the other?
- What counts for more in development exercises like this—good economics or good politics?
- Do you regard the motor launches and the fish processing plant as "appropriate" technological developments for Alpha and Beta? Explain the meaning of "appropriate" in this context.
- What account should be taken in project organization of the reported schism between the communities of Alpha and Beta? How serious is the risk that this difference will thwart plans?

People Versus Planners

- Do the people of Alpha and Beta currently have enough say in plans for their development?
- Should their influence over the project be increased or curtailed? How should this be done?
- Which people *within* these two communities have the most influence over development decisions? Do they stand to benefit unfairly? How—if necessary—should their influence be moderated?
- What risk is there that extending the influence of local people over decisions will actually weaken development efforts?
- What appears to be the current relationship between the people of Alpha and Beta and the officials who are seeking to develop these communities? Does this relationship bode well or badly for the project?

Local Interests Versus National Interests

- How is the project likely to benefit Arcadians *outside* the two communities?
- Will these external benefits prove costly to the people of Alpha and Beta themselves?

Individual Opportunity and Collective Responsibility

- It is proposed that the Alpha-Beta project will be managed by the local branch of the National Fishermen's Cooperative Union. Is this wise?
- What alternative form of management might you suggest?
- What are the most serious problems to be confronted in (re)organizing this cooperative? How should these problems be solved?
- Does the project offer adequate opportunities for individual advancement?

Matters Arising

Finally, when you have made your proposal and—ideally—discussed it with colleagues, you may care to reflect on the whole Arcadian spoof.

- How would *you* have set up the game? What would make it work more effectively, as an evocation of "real" development issues, as a learning exercise, and as a game that gets players interested and involved?
- What sort of country, government, community, and so on would have made a more satisfactory basis for this sort of exercise? Why?
- Dream up a community or a society of your own in which people are so content that interventions of the sort proposed in this book are unnecessary. Is such an ideal practicable? Is it the sort of vision that any of the actors in this project, including yourself, have been pursuing? What would it take to realize such an ideal? Would you yourself like to live in such a world?
- Real intellectual growth depends at least as much on posing stimulating questions as on devising plausible answers. Go through this final section of the book and add questions of your own. I would like to think that by the time you are finished, the spacious margins will be as busy as the text.

Reading Guide

This selection of readings is intended both as a guide to the issues raised in these documents and as a general introduction to social issues of development. Texts are arranged under a series of (overlapping) headings according to topics the reader may wish to pursue.

Poverty, Inequality, and Progress

Chambers, Robert. 1983. *Rural Development: Putting the Last First*. London: Longman.

Dunn, John. 1993. *Western Political Theory in the Face of the Future*. Cambridge: Cambridge University Press.

George, Susan, and Paige, Nigel. 1982. *Food for Beginners*. London: Writers and Readers Publishing Cooperative.

Lappé, F., and Collins, J. 1977. *Food First: Beyond the Myth of Scarcity*. Boston: Houghton Mifflin.

Lawrence, Peter. 1987. *World Recession and the Food Crisis in Africa*. Boulder, Colo.: Westview Press.

Lipton, Michael. 1977. *Why Poor People Stay Poor: Urban Bias in World Development*. London: Maurice Temple Smith.

Nussbaum, Martha, and Sen, Amartya, eds. 1993. *The Quality of Life*. Oxford: Clarendon Press.

Schultz, Theodore W. 1993. *The Economics of Being Poor*. Oxford: Blackwell.

Sen, Amartya. 1981. *Poverty and Famines: An Essay on Entitlement and Deprivation*. Oxford: Clarendon Press.

Techniques and Politics

Bernard, H. Russell, and Pelto, Pertti, eds. 1987. *Technology and Social Change*. Prospect Heights, Ill.: Waveland Press.

Dahl, Gudrun, ed. 1993. *Green Arguments and Local Subsistence*. Stockholm: Department of Social Anthropology, Stockholm University.

Pfaffenberger, Bryan. 1992. "Social Anthropology of Technology." *Annual Review of Anthropology* 21: 491–516.

Rybczynski, Witold. 1980. *Paper Heroes: A Review of Appropriate Technology*. New York: Anchor Books.

Schumacher, E. F. 1973. *Small Is Beautiful: A Study of Economics as if People Mattered*. London: Blond & Briggs.

Smillie, Ian. 1991. *Mastering the Machine: Poverty, Aid and Technology*. Boulder, Colo.: Westview Press.

Fishing and Social Organization

Acheson, James M. 1981. "Anthropology of Fishing." *Annual Review of Anthropology* 10: 275–316.

Firth, Raymond. 1966. *Malay Fishermen: Their Peasant Economy*. London: Routledge.

Lewis, Norman. 1985. *Voices of the Old Sea*. Harmondsworth, England: Penguin.

Maiolo, John R., and Orbach, Michael. 1982. *Modernization and Marine Fisheries Policy*. Ann Arbor, Mich.: Ann Arbor Science Publishers.

Pollnac, Richard B. 1991. "Social and Cultural Characteristics in Small-scale Fishery Development." In Michael Cernea, ed., *Putting People First*. Second ed. New York: Oxford University Press, pp. 189–223.

Individual Opportunity and Collective Responsibility

Attwood, D. W., and Baviskar, B. S., eds. 1988. *Who Shares? Co-operatives and Rural Development*. New Delhi: Oxford University Press.

Dorner, P., ed. 1977. *Cooperative and Commune*. Madison: University of Wisconsin Press.

Hardin, Garret, and Baden, J., eds. 1987. *Managing the Commons*. San Fransisco: W. H. Freeman.

Worsley, Peter, ed. 1971. *Two Blades of Grass: Rural Cooperatives in Agricultural Modernization*. Manchester: Manchester University Press.

Women and Development

Afshar, Haleh. 1985. *Women, Work and Ideology in the Third World*. London: Tavistock.

Boserup, Ester. 1970. *Woman's Role in Economic Development*. London: George Allen & Unwin.

Charlton, Sue Ellen M. 1984. *Women in Third World Development*. Boulder, Colo.: Westview Press.

Dauber, Roslyn R., and Cain, Melinda L., eds. 1981. *Women and Technological Change in Developing Countries*. Boulder, Colo.: Westview Press.

Moore, Henrietta L. 1988. *Feminism and Anthropology*. Cambridge: Polity Press.

Moser, Caroline O. N. 1993. *Gender Planning and Development: Theory, Practice and Training*. London: Routledge.

Rogers, Barbara. 1980. *The Domestication of Women: Discrimination in Developing Societies*. New York: St. Martin's Press.

Tinker, Irene, ed. 1990. *Persistent Inequalities: Women and World Development*. New York: Oxford University Press.

Perceptions of Development

Brody, Hugh. 1983. *Maps and Dreams: Indians and the British Columbia Frontier*. Harmondsworth, England: Penguin.

Dahl, Gudrun, and Rabo, Annika, eds. 1992. *Kam-ap or Take-off: Local Notions of Development*. Stockholm: Stockholm University.

Ferguson, James. 1990. *The Anti-politics Machine: "Development," Depoliticization, and Bureaucratic Power in Lesotho*. Cambridge: Cambridge University Press.

Lea, John. 1988. *Tourism and Development in the Third World*. London: Routledge.

Richards, Paul. 1985. *Indigenous Agricultural Revolution: Ecology and Food Production in West Africa*. Boulder, Colo: Westview Press.

Wallman, Sandra, ed. 1977. *Perceptions of Development*. Cambridge: Cambridge University Press.

People and Planners

Ellman, Michael. 1989. *Socialist Planning*. Cambridge: Cambridge University Press.

Hall, Anthony, and Midgley, James. 1988. *Development Policies: Sociological Perspectives*. Manchester: Manchester University Press.

Long, Norman. 1989. *An Introduction to the Sociology of Rural Development*. Boulder, Colo.: Westview Press.

Robertson, A. F. 1984. *People and the State: An Anthropology of Planned Development*. Cambridge: Cambridge University Press.

Selznick, P. 1966. *TVA and the Grass Roots: A Study in the Sociology of Formal Organization*. Berkeley: University of California Press.

Local Interests in the
Political Economy of the Modern World

Bodley, John H. 1990. *Victims of Progress.* Mountain View, Calif.: Mayfield.

Hoogvelt, Ankie M. M. 1982. *The Third World in Global Development.* London: Macmillan.

Rothenstein, F. A., and Blim, M., eds. 1992. *Anthropology and the Global Factory.* New York: Bergin & Garvey.

Seligson, Mitchell A., and Passe-Smith, John T., eds. 1993. *Development and Underdevelopment: The Political Economy of Inequality.* Boulder, Colo.: Lynne Rienner.

Sklair, Leslie, ed. 1994. *Capitalism and Development.* London: Routledge.

Toye, John F. J. 1993. *Dilemmas of Development: Reflections on the Counter-revolution in Development Theory and Policy.* Oxford: Blackwell.

Wolf, Eric. 1982. *Europe and the People Without History.* Berkeley: University of California Press.

World Bank. Annual editions. *World Development Report.* New York: Oxford University Press.

Worsley, Peter. 1984 *The Three Worlds: Culture and World Development.* Chicago: University of Chicago Press.

Social Research and Assessment

Cernea, Michael, ed. 1991. *Putting People First: Sociological Variables in Rural Development.* Second ed. New York: Oxford University Press.

Derman, William, and Whiteford, Scott, eds. 1985. *Social Impact Analysis and Development Planning in the Third World.* Boulder, Colo.: Westview Press.

Devereux, Stephen, and Hoddinott, John, eds. 1993. *Fieldwork in Developing Countries.* Boulder, Colo.: Lynne Rienner.

Finsterbusch, Kurt; Ingersoll, Jasper; and Llewellyn, Lynn; eds. 1990. *Methods for Social Analysis in Developing Countries.* Boulder, Colo.: Westview Press.

Pottier, Johan. 1993. *Practising Development: Social Science Perspectives.* London: Routledge.